Free movement of judgements within the EU:

abolishment of the exequatur and

reform of the grounds of refusal to enforce?

-

The Commission's proposal for a new Brussels I Regulation

Bibliografische Information der Deutschen Nationalbibliothek
Die Deutsche Nationalbibliothek verzeichnet diese Publikation in der Deutschen Nationalbibliografie; detaillierte bibliografische Daten sind im Internet über http://dnb.d-nb.de abrufbar.
1. Aufl. - Göttingen : Cuvillier, 2011
Zugl.: Nottingham, Univ., Diss., 2011

978-3-86955-984-1

Nonnenstieg 8, 37075 Göttingen
Telefon: 0551-54724-0
Telefax: 0551-54724-21
www.cuvillier.de

1. Auflage, 2011
Gedruckt auf säurefreiem Papier

978-3-86955-984-1

Preface

This paper was originally submitted as a thesis in completion of the LL.M. programme in International Commercial Law at the University of Nottingham, United Kingdom.

I would like to extent my appreciation to Prof. James J. Fawcett for encouraging and supervising this thesis. Moreover, I would like to thank my friends and colleagues at the School of Law who made my year in the United Kingdom an unforgettable experience. Special mention should be made for my friend Vasyl Chornyi for many hours of discussions and inspiring new ideas, and Jennifer Marie-Luise Wackwitz for her constant support.

The work reflects the state of law on 7 September 2011.

Berlin, December 2011 Christoph Kirsch

Outline

A. Introduction

Among the existing instruments on European international civil procedure, the Regulation 44/2001 ('Brussels I')[1] which came into force on 1 March 2002 is certainly the most important one.[2] It has the widest scope covering almost all civil and commercial matters and concerns the most important questions of international civil litigation, namely heads of jurisdiction and recognition and enforcement of judgments given in another Member State (except Denmark).[3] Brussels I is one of the most successful pieces of European legislation.[4] However, only a week before the regulation's eighth anniversary the Commission presented its reform proposal on 14 December 2010 ('the Proposal').[5] Despite the success of Brussels I the Proposal will result in considerable changes, should it be realised in its current form. Against the background that European law guarantees economic freedoms[6] cross-border recognition and enforcement of judgments within the European Union ('EU') is of considerable and increasing importance. Brussels I continued the project started by its predecessor, the Brussels Convention 1968,[7] with the final aim of free movement of judgments (recital 6) within the European Union as a single area of freedom, security and jus-

---

1 Council Regulation (EC) No 44/2001 of 22 December 2000 on jurisdiction and the recognition and enforcement of judgments in civil and commercial matters [2001] OJ L 12/1(hereinafter: 'Brussels I').

2 Magnus/Mankowski/*Magnus*, Introduction para. 12, for the main currently existing instruments cf. para. 10.

3 Art. 1(3) Brussels I and recital 21 in accordance with Protocol No 22 on the position of Denmark [2008] OJ C 115/299. For the relations between the EU and Denmark cf. the Agreement between the European Community and the Kingdom of Denmark on jurisdiction and the recognition and enforcement of judgments in civil and commercial matters, [2005] OJ L 299/62.

4 European Parliament resolution of 7 September 2010 on the implementation and review of Council Regulation (EC) No 44/2001 on jurisdiction and the recognition and enforcement of judgments in civil and commercial matters (P7_TA(2010)0304), available at: http://www.europarl.europa.eu/sides/getDoc.do?pubRef=-//EP//NONSGML+TA+P7-TA-2010-0304+0+DOC+PDF+V0//EN (last accessed: 03.07.2011) (hereinafter 'Resolution of 7 September 2010'), recital A.

5 Proposal for a Regulation of the European Parliament and of the Council on jurisdiction and the recognition and enforcement of judgments in civil and commercial matters, COM(2010) 748 final.

6 For these so-called "four freedoms" see Art. 21, 28 et seqq., 45, 49 et seqq., 56 et seqq., 63 et seqq. TFEU.

7 Convention on Jurisdiction and the Enforcement of Judgments in Civil and Commercial Matters of 1968, (consolidated version) [1998] OJ C 27/1 (hereinafter 'Brussels Convention').

tice.[8] *Inter alia* it provides for a simplified and accelerated procedure to obtain the required declaration of enforceability (*the exequatur*) in the Member State of enforcement. Now the general abolishment of this exequatur lies at the heart of the Proposal. It is accompanied by plans to reform the existing defences. However, reforms should be accepted only if they improve the *status quo* considering the relevant interests, and if they are justified by practical needs. That may conflict with the political aim at European level but reforms are expensive and, if proposed for the mere sake of novelty, they could unnecessarily interfere with the well established structure and principles of Brussels I.

This paper analyses and discusses the most relevant aspects of the abolishment of the exequatur and the reform of the defences under the Proposal. First, the background on the preparation of the Proposal and its underlying principles will be provided in chapter A. In chapter B the cross-border enforcement regimes of Brussels I and the Proposal will be presented. Then the abolishment of the exequatur will be critically discussed with regard to its underlying rationales and the functions of the exequatur. The chapter concludes with the implications of the abolishment for the existing defences. The reform of the defences is discussed in Chapter C. It will be analysed whether the relevant Proposal provisions provide sufficient protection and comply with the principle of mutual recognition. Particular emphasis is put on the *ordre public* defence and its fundamental rights implications. Finally, suggestions to amend the Proposal are made throughout the paper.

---

[8] Art. 3(2) Treaty on European Union (consolidated version) [2010] OJ C 83/13 (hereinafter 'TEU'), Art. 67-89 The Treaty on the Functioning of the European Union (consolidated version) [2010] OJ C 83/47 (hereinafter 'TFEU').

B. Background: review and reform of the Brussels I Regulation

Art. 73 Brussels I obliged the Commission to present a report on the application of the Regulation five years after its entry into force, i.e. in 1 March 2007. In preparing this report the Commission took into account several external studies,[9] most notably for the purpose of this paper, a study by *Hess*, *Pfeiffer* and *Schlosser* on the practical application of Brussels I – the *Heidelberg Report* (2007)[10] – based *inter alia* on national reports of the Member States.[11] With considerable delay the Commission presented its Report on Brussels I[12] together with a Green Paper[13] in April 2009. According to the Report the regulation is very successful and highly appreciated among practitioners with, however, room for improvements.[14] The Green Paper identified specific aspects where improvements are conceivable and initiated a consultation[15] of the interested public which resulted in a total of 130 responses.[16] The European Parliament passed a resolution on the implementation and review of Brussels I in 7 September 2010.[17] On the basis of these extensive preparatory works the Commission finally presented its Proposal for a new regulation in 14 December 2010. It is accompanied by an Explanatory Memorandum[18] stating the reasons for the reform

---

9 Cf. Explanatory Memorandum to the Proposal for a Regulation of the European Parliament and of the Council on jurisdiction and the recognition and enforcement of judgments in civil and commercial matters (hereinafter 'Explanatory Memorandum'), COM(2010) 748 final, para. 2 with further reference.

10 For a revised version of this study cf. *Hess/Pfeiffer/Schlosser*, Heidelberg Report.

11 Available at: http://ec.europa.eu/justice/civil/document/index_en.htm (last accessed: 01.07.2011).

12 Report from the Commission to the European Parliament, the Council and the European Economic and Social Committee on the application of Council Regulation (EC) No 44/2001 on Jurisdiction and the recognition and enforcement of judgments in civil and commercial matters (21.04.2009) (hereinafter 'The Report'), COM(2009) 174 final.

13 Green Paper on the review of Council Regulation (EC) No 44/2001 on Jurisdiction and the recognition and enforcement of judgments in civil and commercial matters (21.04.2009) (hereinafter 'The Green Paper'), COM(2009) 175 final.

14 The Report, COM(2009) 175 final, para. 2.2.

15 For the questions concerning the abolishment of the exequatur, The Green Paper, COM(2009) 175 final, p. 3.

16 Available at: http://ec.europa.eu/justice/news/consulting_public/news_consulting_0002_en.htm (last accessed 01.07.2011).

17 European Parliament, Resolution of 7 September 2010 (P7_TA(2010)0304).

18 COM(2010) 748 final.

proposals and an Impact Assessment[19] analysing the costs and benefits of their main aspects. The legal basis of the new regulation is Art. 81(2)(a), (c), and (e) TFEU and its adoption has to follow the ordinary legislative procedure of Art. 289(1), 294 TFEU. Fortunately, from a European perspective, the United Kingdom (UK) and Ireland confirmed their participation in the reform in accordance with Protocol 21[20] in April 2011.[21]

Since the Treaty of Amsterdam (1997) the creation of the area of freedom, security and justice is an important field of European policy implying the application of the techniques of integration to European civil procedural law.[22] In the presidency conclusion of the Tampere Summit 1999 the European Council declared the principle of mutual recognition the "cornerstone of judicial co-operation" within the EU.[23] With the Treaty of Lisbon this principle is now expressed in the Treaty.[24] Thus, corresponding to the European Council's Stockholm Programme (2009),[25] the Commission's reform objective is to facilitate cross-border litigation and the free movement of judgments in line with the principle of mutual recognition.[26] Although the proposed reform comprises several elements,[27] the abolishment of exequatur plays the central role in the Proposal. On 26 June 2011 the European Parliament presented a draft report on the

---

19 Commission Staff Working Paper – Impact Assessment – Accompanying document to the Proposal for a regulation of the European Parliament and of the Council on jurisdiction and the recognition and enforcement of judgments in civil and commercial matters (Recast), 14.12.2010 (hereinafter 'Impact Assessment'), SEC(2010) 1547 final.

20 Protocol (No 21) on the position of the United Kingdom and Ireland in respect of the Area of Freedom, Security and Justice [2010] OJ C 83/295.

21 Cf. *Bar Council*, Brussels News June 2011, available at: http://www.barcouncil.org.uk/aboutthebar council/BrusselsOffice/BrusselsNewsJune2011/ (last accessed: 03.07. 2011).

22 Cf. *Hess/Pfeiffer/Schlosser*, Heidelberg Report, para. 61.

23 European Council, Tampere European Council (15./16.10.1999), Presidency Conclusions, available at: http://www.europarl.europa.eu/summits/tam_en.htm (last accessed: 03.07.2011), (hereinafter 'Tampere Conclusions'), para. 33.

24 Concerning civil matters: Art. 67(4), 81(1), (2)(a) TFEU.

25 European Council, The Stockholm Programme – An open and secure Europe serving and protecting the citizens (10./11.12.2009), OJ 2010 C 115/1 (hereinafter 'Stockholm Programme'), p. 13.

26 Explanatory Memorandum, COM(2010) 748 final, para. 1.2.; cf. also Communication from the Commission to the European Parliament, the Council, the European Economic and Social Committee and the Committee of the Regions – Delivering an area of freedom, security and justice for Europe's citizens – Action Plan Implementing the Stockholm Programme, COM(2010) 171, p. 19.

27 Cf. Explanatory Memorandum, COM(2010) 748 final, para. 3.1.; also *Carruthers*, SLT 2011, p. 31 et seqq.

Commission's Proposal with a Parliament Resolution recommending several amendments and accompanied by an explanatory statement.[28]

[28] EU Parliament – Committee on Legal Affairs, Draft Report 2010/0383(COD) (26.06.2011).

C. Abolishment of the exequatur requirement

An assessment of the proposal to abolish the exequatur first requires an overview of the systems for the enforcement of foreign judgments under Brussels I and the Proposal. Subsequently the abolishment will be critically discussed with reference to its underlying rationales, similar regimes in other instruments and the functions of the exequatur.

I. Enforcement under Brussels I – the exequatur requirement

Under Brussels I judgments within the wide meaning of Art. 32 given in a Member State in respect of matters within the scope of the Regulation,[29] although automatically recognised in any other Member State (Art. 33(1)), are not automatically enforceable there. Art. 38(1) requires a declaration of enforceability, the so-called *exequatur*,[30] which is a remainder of the Member State's sovereignty. The exequatur procedure under Brussels I consists of the application for the exequatur and a possible appeal stage. The exequatur imports the foreign title in the legal system of the Member State. Not the foreign title but the exequatur is the basis of enforcement.[31] The exequatur procedure in Brussels I must be distinguished from the actual enforcement in the Member State because the latter is not covered by the regulation and therefore governed by the respective national law.[32]

The exequatur is granted upon a without notice application of any interested party (Art. 38(1)) to the court or competent authority listed in Annex II (Art. 39(1))[33] immediately after the authenticity of the judgment has been established, Art. 41. Therefore, the application must provide the documents required under

---

[29] Art. 1(1) requires a *civil and commercial matter*, for this term cf. Case 29/76 *Lufttransportunternehmen GmbH & Co. KG v Eurocontrol* [1976] ECR I-1541, para. 4; Art. 1(1), (2) list excluded matters.

[30] This is the most common use of the term 'exequatur' also followed by the Proposal, cf. Explanatory Memorandum, para. 3.1.1. If the enforcement Member State is the UK the judgment has to be registered for enforcement in the relevant part (i.e. England and Wales, Scotland, or Northern Ireland), Art. 38(2) Brussels I.

[31] Cf. Rauscher/*Mankowski*, Art. 38 Brussels I para. 3.; *Bach*, ZRP 2011, p. 98.

[32] Case 148/84 Deutsche Genossenschaftsbank v Brasserie du pêcheur SA [1985] ECR I-1981, para. 13.

[33] In England: the High Court, in Germany: the presiding judge of a chamber of the 'Landgericht'.

Art. 40(3): a copy of the judgment, a certificate on its enforceability in the Member State of origin, and a translation of the documents if requested (Art. 53, 54, 55(2)). Where Brussels I provides no special rules, the procedure for making the application is governed by the law of the enforcement state, Art. 40(1).[34] Without notice and the possibility for the debtor to make any submissions (Art. 41) the first stage is an *ex parte* procedure with purely formal checks. Hence, the procedure for obtaining the exequatur is simple and prevents the judgment debtor from removing assets out of the jurisdiction in order to thwart the applicant.[35] The debtor is not seriously prejudiced because during the time for an appeal (second stage) actual enforcement proceedings are limited to protective measures, Art. 47(3), 43(5).

In contrast to the Brussels Convention, only in the adversarial procedure at the appeal stage the limited grounds for revoking the exequatur specified in Art. 34, 35 (the 'defences') can be invoked, without however, allowing a review of the judgment as to its substance (*révision au fond*), Art. 45. The defences are discussed in detail in chapter C.

II. Enforcement under the Commission's Proposal

The Proposal contains the relevant provisions on enforceability and enforcement in Chapter III (Art. 37-69). Its structure is generally more complex as a consequence of the adoption of two parallel regimes in Section 1 and 2 (Art. 37(2), (3)) with common provisions in Section 3. For judgments within Section 1, i.e. within the meaning of Art. 2(a) except those to which Section 2 applies, Art. 38(2) abolishes the exequatur. As soon as such a judgment is enforceable in the Member State of origin it is directly enforceable in any other Member State. Hence, it is *ex lege* treated like a domestic judgment without any formal checks. The creditor must turn directly to the competent enforcement authority. However, it is still necessary to distinguish enforceability and actual enforcement. The latter is governed by the national laws (Art. 41(1)) and the creditor must still provide documents to establish the authenticity and enforceability of the judgment (Art. 42(1), (2) and Annex I). The competent authority can request a translation of the Annex I certificate on enforceability but, in principle, not of the judgment anymore, Art. 42(3), (4). The extended certificate is supposed to provide the authority with the information necessary to enforce the judgment. A

[34] Cf. Civil Jurisdiction and Judgments Order, SI 2001/3929, Art. 3 and Sch.1, para. 2 and CPR, Part 74.2-74.7.

[35] Cf. Case 125/79 *Denilauler v SNC Couchet Frèreres* [1980] ECR I-1553, para. 14.

creditor can immediately avail himself of any protective measure available under the law of the enforcement state (Art. 40) and the debtor is provided with special remedies against the enforcement in Art. 43, 45 and 46.

According to Art. 37(3) the described regime does not apply to judgments concerning (a) non-contractual obligations arising from violations of privacy rights relating to personality, including defamation, and (b) obligations for collective redress. Apart from minor adjustments,[36] Section 2 (Art. 47-63) maintains the current Brussels I regime for those judgments. The Commission justifies this with a lack of the necessary mutual trust in respect of the matters concerned which is due to insufficient harmonisation and strongly diverging approaches adopted by the Member States at the national level.[37] A detailed analysis of this exception is beyond the scope of this paper. Suffice it to note the criticism *inter alia* by the European Parliament for causing legal uncertainty.[38]

III. Discussion of the Proposal: Should the exequatur be abolished?

The Commission bases the abolishment of the exequatur on "mutual trust in the administration of justice in the Union and the aim of making cross-border litigation less time consuming and costly".[39] These rationales need to be analysed. Moreover the functions of the exequatur and the practical implications of an abolishment will be considered.

1. The political rationale: mutual trust

The principle of mutual trust was already the basis of the exequatur procedures established by the Brussels Convention and Brussels I, and has been employed by the Court of Justice ('ECJ') in its case law.[40] Thus the abolishment of the ex-

---

36 *Inter alia* Art. 53(2) limits the option to request a translation, and the number of defences is reduced, Art. 48.

37 Explanatory Memorandum, COM(2010) 748 final, para. 3.1.1.

38 European Parliament - Committee on Legal Affairs, Draft Report on the proposal for a regulation of the European Parliament and of the Council on jurisdiction and the recognition and enforcement of judgments in civil and commercial matters (recast) (26.06.2011) (hereinafter 'Draft Report of 26 June 2011'), 2010/0383(COD), p. 47.

39 Recital 23 of the Proposal. Cf. also Explanatory Memorandum, COM(2010) 748 final, para. 3.1.1.

40 Cf. Jenard-Report [1979] OJ C 59/1, p.46; Recitals 17 Brussels I; Case C-116/02 *Erich Gasser GmbH v Misat Srl.* [2004] ECR I-14693, para. 72; Case C-159/02 *Turner v Grovit* [2005] ECR I-3565, para. 24.

equatur seems to necessitate an even higher degree of mutual trust between the Member States. The wording of recital 23 Proposal suggests its existence without stating any reason. One reason could be that all Member States acceded to the European Convention on Human Rights (ECHR). Hence, their civil procedures must comply with the guarantees of Art. 6 ECHR.[41] Another reason could be that the legal systems of all Member States are characterised by the principles of democracy, the protection of human rights and the rule of law.[42] However, despite these commonalities in principle their actual implementation in the Member States still differs. *Sujecki* provides an example of a case in which different results are reached within the framework of Art. 6 ECHR.[43] Under German civil procedure law the claim form must be served with all annexes referred to therein, otherwise the service is generally void.[44] Not so under Dutch civil procedure law, where the claimant is only precluded from relying on information contained in the missing annex.[45] This demonstrates how diversely Art. 6 ECHR is implemented in the Member States potentially leading to different results. Similarities of the legal systems cannot be denied but it seems critical in the light of the existing differences that the Commission naturally relies on mutual trust. With their repeated reference the European institutions have elevated mutual trust to a core principle of European civil procedure law.[46] Yet, trust in the administration of justice in the other States cannot be imposed but rather evolves from experience. Thus, rather than a rationale, the Commission's recourse appears as a postulate, a fiction used to achieve the aim of free movement of judgments.[47] The European legislator even seems to acknowledge this with the partial procedural harmonisation in some regulations relating to special matters.[48] On the other hand, the facilitation of this aim indeed requires mutual trust. The legal environment of the Member States is too complex to be entirely evaluated beforehand so that there is always some uncertainty involved. Hence, each stage of integration towards the single area of justice requires all partici-

---

41 Due to only very partial harmonisation of the civil procedure laws EU fundamental rights are less relevant in this respect because they are binding only for acts within the scope of application of EU law, cf. Case 5/88 *Wachauf v Germany* [1989] ECR 2609, para. 19; *Chalmers/Davies/Monti*, EU Law, p. 253.

42 Cf. *Wagner*, IPRax 2002, p. 91; *Georganti*, Ordre public, p. 138

43 Cf. *Sujecki*, ZEuP 2008, p. 468 et seq.

44 § 253(1) ZPO; BGH (German Federal Court of Justice) EuZW 2007, 187, para. 13.

45 Art. 85(1) Wetboek van Burgerlijke Rechtsvordering (Dutch Civil Procedure Code).

46 Cf. *Blobel/Späth*, ELRev 2005, p. 540; *Fabian*, Europäische Mahnverordnung, p. 299.

47 Also *Sujecki*, ZEuP 2008, p. 469; *Blobel/Späth*, ELRev 2005, p. 535; *Rauscher*, Europäischer Vollstreckungstitel, p. 7.

48 Cf. *inter alia* Art. 12-18 Regulation (EC) No 805/2004 [2004] OJ L 134/15.

pants to make "a leap in the dark".[49] For *Cuniberti* and *Rueda* the free movement of judgments is an end in itself.[50] This seems more realistic; demanding mutual trust to achieve the final aim rather than purporting its existence. On the other hand, the success of the Brussels Convention and Brussels I appears as "self-fulfilling prophecy" for they were also based on the postulate of mutual trust.[51] Thus actual trust may be justified by this experience. Finally, given the limited formal check preceding the exequatur under Brussels I the issue of mutual trust seems to be less relevant at this formal stage but rather when it comes to the reform of the defences.

2. The economic rationale: costs and duration

The Commission also points out the duration and costs of the exequatur procedure to justify its abolishment. In theory Brussels I provides for a simple and rapid exequatur procedure and thus largely guarantees the free movement of judgments. The purely formal check should not result in a considerable obstacle. However, the efficiency of the procedure in practice depends on the implementation in the Member States. Moreover, the mere existence of an intermediate procedure makes cross-border litigation more cumbersome than national litigation. It is perceived as discrimination of foreign titles and thus as incompatible with the aim of a single judicial area in which judgments can freely circulate.[52] That is not *per se* convincing because European law generally allows discriminations to be justified.[53] Nevertheless, from around 10,000 applications for an exequatur per year about 93% are successful without an appeal, i.e. the exequatur procedure is a pure formality.[54] Only 1-5% of the exequatur decisions are

---

[49] *Blobel/Späth*, ELRev 2005, p. 540; *Kohler* in Reichelt/Rechberger, Europäischer Kollisionsrecht, p. 75.

[50] *Cuniberti/Rueda*, RabelsZ 2011, p. 292.

[51] *Oberhammer*, JBl. 2006, p. 480.

[52] *Magnus/Mankowski*, ZVglRWiss 109 (2010), p. 2; cf. also *Leible*, ecolex 2011, p. 708.

[53] For the 'four freedoms': Art. 36, 45(3), 52(1), 62, 65(1) TFEU; with respect to Art. 18 TFEU for direct and indirect discriminations arguably Case C-524/06 *Heinz Huber v Germany* [2008] ECR I-9705, paras. 74 et seq.

[54] Figures of 2009, cf. Impact Assessment, SEC(2010) 1547 final, p. 13 and Annex IV A at p. 53.

appealed and rarely successful.[55] This is the background for considering costs and duration of the exequatur procedure.

According to the *Impact Assessment* the realistic overall costs of exequatur proceedings in the EU amount to almost €48 million per year with considerably varying individual costs in the Member States.[56] The average of €2,200 for processing the application includes court and lawyer's fees and costs for translations and service of documents. Despite the exceptional character of Art. 55(2) Brussels I most courts regularly require a translation of the judgment thus unnecessarily raising the costs.[57] Yet, this problem could be sufficiently solved with an extended standard form certificate including the judgment's operative part, and by excluding the right to request a translation of the entire judgment. Since the judgment must not be reviewed as to its substance, the latter is dispensable. As seen above, the Proposal adopts a very similar approach. However, the most compelling costs aspect is the representation by a lawyer in the enforcement state. Although not mandatory, he is regularly needed for preparing the documents and handling the procedure abroad. Creditors usually do not dispose of sufficient information about the exequatur procedure which has been implemented quite differently in the national laws of the Member States.[58] These costs can only be significantly reduced by abolishing the exequatur, even though they will not be eliminated entirely because the actual enforcement is still governed by the foreign national law.

The time for obtaining the exequatur at first instance also varies strongly between the Member States, ranging from a few days up to seven months, not considering the time for preparing the application.[59] In case of an appeal the delay of enforcement even increases up to two years.[60] Against the background of the narrow formal check it is unlikely that the introduction of deadlines would result in improvement because the issue seems to be the capacity of the administration of justice in the respective states.

---

[55] *Hess/Pfeiffer/Schlosser*, Heidelberg Report, paras. 51, 447. The remaining applications are refused at first instance because they do not comply with formal requirements or fall outside the scope of Brussels I.

[56] SEC(2010) 1547 final, p. 14 and Annex IV A at p. 57 stating e.g. Bulgaria: €1,100, UK: €4,000.

[57] *Hess/Pfeiffer/Schlosser*, Heidelberg Report, para. 455.

[58] Ibid. para.458; see also *Oberhammer*, JBl. 2006, p. 484.

[59] Cf. *Hess/Pfeiffer/Schlosser*, Heidelberg Report, para. 456; Impact Assessment, SEC(2010) 1547 final, p. 13 and Annex V at p. 59 et seq.; e.g. England/Wales: 1-3 weeks, Germany: 3 weeks, Greece: 10 days-7 months.

[60] Impact Assessment, SEC(2010) 1547 final, p. 14 and Annex V at p. 60 et seq.

It can be concluded that, although in most cases a pure formality, the procedure for obtaining the exequatur entails considerable costs and (possibly) time. Cross-border litigation often deters businesses from engaging in cross-border trade and becomes even less attractive with the exequatur procedure.[61] Hence, the Commission puts forward strong economic arguments for the abolishment of the exequatur.

3. Abolishment of the exequatur in other legal instruments

Following the Tampere Summit 1999 the Council and the Commission adopted a Programme on Mutual Recognition in 2000 ('2000 Programme') which described their plan to gradually abolish intermediate measures, i.e. *any* check on the foreign judgment in the enforcement State.[62] From 2003 to 2009 a series of regulations for certain judgments was adopted in which the exequatur requirement was "abolished". The Commission now presents these as role models for the Proposal.[63]

The first one, Regulation 2201/2003[64] abolished the exequatur for Member State judgments which concern the right of access or the return of abducted children, and have been specifically certified.[65] However, the actual 'pilot project' of the new European policy was Regulation 805/2004[66] which provides an optional regime allowing a domestic judgment concerning an uncontested claim to be certified as a European Enforcement Order ('EEO') by the court of origin, i.e. as enforceable throughout the EU, Art. 5. Although, there is no need for an exequatur in the enforcement state the certification still functions as a *quasi* ex-

---

61 Ibid., currently only 25% of the European Small and Medium Enterprises engage in cross-border trade.

62 2000 Programme [2001] OJ C 12/01, p. 5, 7.

63 The Green Paper, COM(2009) 175 final, p. 2 et seq.

64 Council Regulation (EC) No 2201/2003 of 27 November 2003 concerning jurisdiction and the recognition and enforcement of judgments in matrimonial matters and the matters of parental responsibility [2003] OJ L 338/1, repealing Regulation (EC) No 1347/2000 (hereinafter 'Regulation 2201/2003').

65 Art. 41(1), (2), Annex III and Art. 42(1), (2), Annex IV, cf. Rauscher/*Rauscher*, Art. 41 Brüssel IIa-VO, para. 3.

66 Regulation (EC) No 805/2004 of the European Parliament and of the Council of 21 April 2004 creating a European Enforcement Order for uncontested claims [2004] OJ L 134/15 (hereinafter 'Regulation 805/2004'); for a short introduction *Crifo*, CJQ 2005, p. 207 et seqq.

equatur or "*passeport européen*".[67] Only the procedure is shifted to the state of origin, thus avoiding the need for an exequatur procedure in each enforcement state ("one stop shop"). Whereas under Regulation 805/2004 the EEO is the basis of enforcement, the subsequently created European Order for Payment (Regulation 1896/2006)[68] and a judgment given in a Small Claims Procedure (Regulation 861/2007)[69] provide for genuine European titles, i.e. are *ipso iure* enforceable throughout the EU without an exequatur.[70] The Proposal adopts the latter approach because the enforceable title is the original judgment, i.e. the standard form certificate of Art. 42(1), (2) and Annex I only has informative character. In the field of family law, Regulation 4/2009 extends the same principles to the enforcement of maintenance obligations.[71]

These regulations are evidence that the enforcement of foreign judgments within the EU is possible without an exequatur procedure, practically and in terms of political consensus. However, it may be argued that there is not yet sufficient experience on their operation to extend their principles, especially with the need for careful evaluation emphasised in the Stockholm Programme.[72] Moreover, these regulations are limited to particular subject matters and decisions, thus even a positive experience does not necessarily justify the abolishment of the exequatur in Brussels I with its comprehensive scope. Hence, the existing legal instruments which abolished the exequatur hardly provide a convincing argument. Nevertheless, some of the issues on the Proposal have been discussed in the context of these regulations and can be useful in the further discussion.

---

[67] *Hess*, Europäisches Zivilprozessrecht, p. 100; cf. also *Bach*, ZRP 2011, p. 98; *Sujecki*, ZEuP 2008, p. 475.

[68] Regulation (EC) No 1896/2006 of the European Parliament and of the Council of 12 December 2006 creating a European order for payment procedure [2006] OJ L 399/1; for a short introduction *Fiorini*, ICLQ 2008, p. 454.

[69] Regulation (EC) No 861/2007 of the European Parliament and of the Council of 11 July 2007 establishing a European Small Claims Procedure [2007] OJ L 199/1; for a short introduction *Fiorini*, ICLQ 2008, p. 457.

[70] Art. 19 Regulation 1896/2006, Art. 20 Regulation 861/2007, cf. also *Leible/Freitag*, EU Forderungsbeitreibung, p. 110.

[71] Council Regulation (EC) No 4/2009 of 18 December 2008 on jurisdiction, applicable law, recognition and enforcement of decisions and cooperation in matters relating to maintenance obligations [2009] OJ L 7/1 (hereinafter 'Regulation 4/2009'), cf. Art. 17, 19, 21.

[72] European Council, Stockholm Programme [2010] OJ C 115/1, p. 6.

4. The functions of exequatur and consequences of an abolishment

Based on the rather pragmatic arguments presented so far, the abolishment of the exequatur is generally supported by the European Parliament, the large majority of stakeholders and all Member States.[73] However, before endorsing the abolishment it seems imperative to analyse the consequences in the light of the functions of the exequatur under Brussels I; in other words, whether these functions actually require an exequatur. The two functions of the exequatur are the 'title import function' and the 'title inspection function'.[74]

a) Title import function

Under Brussels I the exequatur imports the foreign title in the legal system of the enforcement state by providing it with the same force and effect as a domestic judgment.[75] In principal, this is necessary because territorial sovereignty prevents a foreign decision from providing the legal basis for acts of domestic enforcement.[76] The enforcement is a core exercise of state power and as such it generally requires an order emanating from the enforcement state.[77] However, the Member States limited their sovereignty in this respect by providing the EU with competence in Art. 81(1)(a) TFEU, to adopt superseding measures which can be regarded as a waiver of the right to require an exequatur.[78]

Nevertheless, it could be argued that a national enforcement agency may not be able to deal with a foreign judgment and should therefore only be confronted with a decision by its national court declaring that decision enforceable. This may seem odd from the perspective of Member States like Austria and Spain where the domestic enforcement law requires a court decision to initiate the en-

---

[73] European Parliament, Resolution of 7 September 2010 (P7_TA(2010)0304), para. 2; Explanatory Memorandum, COM(2010) 748 final, para. 2; for the UK cf. *Ministry of Justice*, Review of the Brussels I Regulation (EC 44/2001) - Comments from the United Kingdom (03.09.2009), available at: http://ec.europa.eu/justice/news/consulting_public/0002/contributions/ms_governments/united_kingdom_en.pdf (last accessed: 18.07.2011), para. 3.

[74] Cf. *Oberhammer*, IPRax 2010, p. 197; *Cuniberti/Rueda*, RabelsZ 2011, p.303; *Hess*, Europäisches Zivilprozessrecht, p. 95.

[75] For the UK cf. Civil Jurisdiction and Judgments Order, SI 2001/3929, Art. 3 and Sch.1, para. 2(2)

[76] Cf. *Cheshire/North/Fawcett*, Private International Law, p. 514.

[77] Cf. *Schack* in FS für Ericinski, forthcoming; *Rauscher*, Internationales Privatrecht, para. 2227.

[78] Adopting the reasoning of Case C-116/02 *Erich Gasser GmbH v Misat Srl.* [2004] ECR I-14693, para. 72.

forcement anyways.[79] However, there are also Member States like Germany where, for example, the application for the attachment of movable property is addressed directly to the bailiff.[80] Instead of an additional court decision a copy of the German judgment rendered with the execution clause (*Vollstreckungsklausel*, § 725 Zivilprozessordnung, ZPO) authorises the bailiff. For foreign judgments the exequatur takes on that function (§ 8 Anerkennungs- und Vollstreckungsausführungsgesetz, AVAG). In case of its abolishment there will be no prior domestic court decision as is already the case when the other regulations apply.[81] Under Art. 42 Proposal the necessary documents shall be provided to the *competent authority*. As seen above, depending on national law that is not necessarily a court.

Wagner and *Beckmann* argue that if the competent authority is not a court serious problems will arise and refer to the German system as an example.[82] Currently, the exequatur is granted by the court only if the respective judgment comes within the scope of Brussels I. The assessment of whether there is a "civil and commercial matter" can be difficult.[83] Since the bailiff's training is basically limited to the rules for the execution in immovable property he is not qualified to assess whether the judgment falls within the scope of the Regulation. This concern presupposes that the Proposal allows the enforcement to be refused by the enforcement authority when the judgment falls outside its scope or relates to a matter exempted by Art. 37(2). In the absence of an express rule in the Proposal this is a matter of interpretation which must be carried out primarily in the light of its purpose.[84] A possible refusal would most likely undermine the positive time saving effect of abolishing the exequatur because a part of its first instance formal check would be maintained. Thus it contradicts the aim of facilitating the free movement of judgments. In addition, Regulation 805/2004 also prevents the enforcement authority from refusing the enforcement because the original judgment falls outside the scope of the regulation. The ascertainment of

---

79 For Austria cf. *Oberhammer*, EBLR, p. 600; for Spain cf. *Correa Delcasso*, EBLR 2006, p. 700, 702.

80 Cf. *Hess/Mack*, EBLR 2006, p. 667.

81 E.g. for Regulation 805/2004 cf. § 1082 ZPO; *Oberhammer*, IPRax 2010, p. 199 seems to have missed these rules.

82 *Wagner/Beckmann*, RIW 2011, p. 47 et seqq.

83 Cf. e.g. Case 814/79 *Netherlands State v Rüffer* [1980] ECR I-3807; Case C-172/91 *Volker Sonntag v Waidmann* [1993] ECR I-1963; also *Cheshire/North/Fawcett*, Private International Law, p.215 with more references.

84 Cf. inter alia Case 12/76 Industrie Tessili Italiana Como v Dunlop AG [1976] ECR I-1473, para. 9.

the requirements of the EEO is reserved for the court of origin and the enforcement authority in the other Member State is bound by its finding.[85] This direct enforceability is also the objective of the general enforcement rules of the Proposal (recital 23). Finally, Art. 20(2) Regulation 805/2004 and Art. 42(1) Proposal are designed very similar and the certificate referred to in Art. 42(1)(b) and Annex I of the Proposal clearly identifies those judgments which are directly enforceable in the view of the original court, thereby preventing confusion. Hence, the Proposal does not allow a review by the enforcement authority as to the scope of the regulation. This equally applies to the issue whether there is a "judgment" in the meaning of Art. 2(a) Proposal and whether it is enforceable in the Member State of origin. Thus the problems indicated by *Wagner* and *Beckmann* will in fact not occur.

Finally, the exequatur currently enables the court in the enforcement state to adopt the foreign judgment making it compatible with its national enforcement law; in Germany, especially with the principle of certainty and clarity.[86] Again, it is argued that a bailiff or comparable enforcement authority without a legal education will not be qualified to perform this adoption.[87] In most cases the adoption concerns the calculation of legal interest, value added tax or the specification of instalments. In this respect, the standard form certificate in Annex I seems to solve this issue. Following the recommendation of the *Heidelberg Report* it adopts the structure of the EEO certificate and requires the determination of these data.[88] Apart from that, judgments for monetary claims are relatively simple and should not provide for cases requiring an adoption. However, the capacity of the standard form may be exceeded if the judgment is for a none-monetary claim, e.g. for an act, an omission or toleration. Whereas the other regulations abolishing the exequatur are, in principle, limited to money claims Brussels I and the Proposal deal with many different types of judgments. Due to the strong divergence of the national enforcement laws with regard to judgments for non-monetary claims a sufficient standardisation appears impossible.[89] According to Art. 66 Proposal the competent authority shall "adapt the measure or

---

[85] Rauscher/*Pabst*, Art. 20 EG-VollstrTitelVO, para. 20; *Kropholler/von Hein*, Art. 21 EuVTVO, para. 8; dissenting: *Rechberger* in FS Leipold, p. 306 argues in case of an obvious violation a refusal must be possible.

[86] Rauscher/*Mankowski*, Art. 38 Brussels I para. 21; *Seidl*, Vollstreckung und Bestimmtheitsgrundsatz, p. 189 et seq.

[87] *Wagner/Beckmann*, RIW 2011, p. 49.

[88] Cf. *Hess/Pfeiffer/Schlosser*, Heidelberg Report, para. 449; also *Hess/Bittmann*, IPRax 2007, p. 280.

[89] Cf. *Hess/Bittmann*, IPRax 2007, p. 280.

order to one known under its own law which has equivalent effects [...] and pursues similar aims and interests" in case the judgment contains a measure or an order unknown in the Member State of enforcement. It is doubtful whether the authority will always be sufficiently qualified to comply with this provision. Therefore, Art. 66 Proposal should be amended as suggested by the European Parliament, allowing the authority or any of the parties to apply to the court of the enforcement state listed in Annex III to clarify how to adapt the measure or order in question.[90]

Hence, it can be concluded that the "title import function" does not require an exequatur. However, in order to fully achieve the functional compensation for its abolishment Art. 66 Proposal should be amended as proposed above.

b) Title inspection function

Under Brussels I the defences of Art. 34, 35 can be raised in the appeal procedure against the granted exequatur, Art. 45. Hence, the exequatur requirement entails a procedure which enables an inspection of the foreign title. However, the defences are not examined *ex officio* but only based on a remedy raised by the debtor and they are also not examined in the first instance proceeding. There is no apparent reason why the exequatur cannot be abolished while maintaining such remedies allowing an inspection of the title. The connection created by the exequatur procedure under Brussels I is not imperative.[91] This is evidenced by the other regulations which provide for a special remedy to oppose enforcement if the foreign judgment under scrutiny is irreconcilable with another decision in the forum.[92] The Proposal basically follows this approach and provides for special remedies in Art. 43, 45, 46 and hence the 'title inspection function' is served even without an exequatur. Instead of a large number of first instance proceedings for the exequatur and a limited number of remedies, there will only be the limited number of remedies which is a clear improvement. Indeed, this partly maintains the delay issue identified above for appeals against the exequatur. The possibility to limit the enforcement to protective measures by raising defences[93] provides an incentive for delaying tactics. However, the proposal addresses this issue in three different ways. It requires the application for the defence of Art.

---

[90] European Parliament, Draft Report of 26 June 2011 (2010/0383(COD)), p. 39; like this *Hess*, IPRax 2011, p. 129.

[91] Like this *Oberhammer*, IPRax 2010, p. 199; *Cuniberti/Rueda*, RabelsZ 2011, p. 303.

[92] Cf. Art. 21 Regulation 805/2004, Art. 22 Regulation 1896/2006, Art. 22 Regulation 861/2007, Art. 21 Regulation 4/2009.

[93] Cf. Art. 47(3) Brussels I and Art. 44(1)(a) Proposal.

45(1) to be dismissed within 30 days if manifestly unfound (Art. 45(5)), and the unsuccessful party of the application of Art. 45(1) to bear the costs of the proceedings (Art. 45(8)).[94] In case of an application under Art. 43 enforcement cannot even be limited to protective measures as Art. 44(1) does not refer to this provision.

IV. Interim conclusion

The previous discussion demonstrated that the Proposal aims at a fundamental change of the European cross-border enforcement system by abolishing the exequatur. Whereas mutual trust does not seem to serve as a reasonable rationale but rather as a postulate, the economic benefits are undeniable. Even with the abolishment the functions of the exequatur are still served as a result of the supplementing reforms, especially the extension of the standard form certificate. Eliminating the formal stage of European cross-border enforcement benefits the creditor and thus provides an incentive for cross-border businesses. At the same time, the debtor's position is not impaired. His interests are rather a matter of the defences available against the enforcement which are the subject of the following chapter. Hence, the abolishment of the exequatur must generally be endorsed. However, Art. 66 Proposal on the adoption of the judgment should be amended to allow the consultation of a court which, at best, may have created a specialist chamber.

[94] For the latter already cf. *Cuniberi/Rueda*, RabelsZ 2011, p. 307.

D. Reform of the defences against the enforcement

Brussels I provides for an exhaustive number of defences in Art. 34 and 35 against the exequatur which can only be raised at the appeal stage in the exequatur procedure, Art. 45(1). According to Art. 45(2) Brussels I the foreign judgment may under no circumstances be reviewed as to its substance (*révision au fond*). However, enforcement of the foreign judgment (or more precisely, the exequatur) shall be refused according to Art. 34: (1) if it is manifestly contrary to public policy in the addressed Member State (*ordre public* defence)[95]; (2) if it is a default judgment and the debtor was insufficiently served (*natural justice* defence); and (3) and (4) in case of irreconcilable judgments. Moreover, according to Art. 35(1) a judgment shall not be enforced if the court of origin assumed jurisdiction contrary to certain heads of jurisdiction under Brussels I, or in a case provided for in Art. 72 (special international agreement prior to the Brussels I).

It was already pointed out at the end of the previous chapter, abolishing the exequatur (procedure) does not necessarily mean that the defences are abolished or that no review can take place in the Member State of enforcement. Unfortunately, some commentators[96] fail to clearly distinguish both questions. Indeed, the procedural framework in which the defences are currently raised would be eliminated. Nevertheless, defences can still be provided *via* the remedies available at the national enforcement law level or by providing for special remedies in the regulation.[97] The Proposal opts for the latter and provides three special remedies in Art. 43, 45 and 46. Therefore, the Commission took into account the numerous recommendations to maintain some safeguards.[98]

Any available defence obviously represents an obstacle to the free movement of judgments within the EU. Before this general objective, it therefore comes as no surprise that the defences have also been subject to reform proposals. This chapter adopts the structure of Art. 34, 35 Brussels I. After a presentation of the

---

[95] The Continental law term 'ordre public' is adopted in this paper to clearly distinguish this concept from the common law 'public policy', for the latter cf. *Cheshire/North/Fawcett*, Private International Law, pp. 139-150, 556-558.

[96] Cf. *inter alia Beaumont/Johnston*, J.Priv.Int.L. 2010, p. 270 et seq.

[97] Cf. also *Oberhammer*, IPRax 2010, p. 199.

[98] Cf. *Hess/Pfeiffer/Schlosser*, Heidelberg Report, para. 729; European Parliament, Resolution of 7 September 2010 (P7_TA(2010)0304), para. 2; Impact Assessment, SEC(2010) 1547 final, p. 19 and Annex II.

basic features of each defence the changes under the Proposal will be identified and subsequently discussed. In line with the academic discussion the clear emphasis will be on the *ordre public* defence – its existence and its content.

I. Ordre Public

1. Art. 34(1) Brussels I Regulation

The wording of Art. 34(1) Brussels I implies that the content of '*ordre public*' depends on the national conception developed by the courts of the State where enforcement is sought. However, as a term of European law its limits are a matter of interpretation in the light of the purpose of Brussels I – the facilitation of the free movement of judgments[99] – and thus subject to review by the ECJ.[100] In *Krombach v Bamberski,* the ECJ restated the exceptional nature of the *ordre public* defence[101] (underscored by the word "manifestly") and defined the narrow limits in which the national courts may have recourse to that concept. Accordingly, the enforcement "would have to constitute a manifest breach of a rule of law regarded as essential in the legal order of the State in which enforcement is sought or of a right recognised as being fundamental within that legal order."[102] Despite being a national concept, the Member States' public policies contain a common core established by fundamental European law principles which may be referred to as 'European *ordre public*'.[103] It follows from *Krombach* that this includes European fundamental rights[104] but not every misapplication of European law represents a breach of an essential rule of law.[105]

Similarly, a difference in the law or the private international law (PIL) rule applied by the court of origin from that, which would have been applied in the Member State of enforcement, or the fact that the court misapplied the law, are

---

99 Recital 6; for the preceding Art. 27(1) Brussels Convention cf. Jenard Report [1979] OJ C 59/1, p. 1.

100 Cf. *Dicey/Morris/Collins*, Conflict of Laws I, para. 14-208; *Layton/Mercer*, EU Civil Practice I, para. 26.014.

101 Case C-7/98 [2000] ECR I-1935, para. 21 citing Case 145/86 *Hoffmann v Krieg* [1988] ECR I-645, para. 21.

102 Case C-7/98 *Krombach v Bamberski* [2000] ECR I-1935, para. 37.

103 Cf. *Meidanis*, ELRev 2005, p. 97, 104; Magnus/Mankowski/*Francq*, Art. 34 para. 15.

104 Ibid. paras. 38-40. The ECJ used Art. 6 ECHR to cast light on the concept of *ordre public*.

105 Case C-38/98 *Régie Nationale Des Usines Renault Sa v Maxicar SpA and Orazio Formento* [2000] ECR I-2973, para. 32, 34; cf. Magnus/Mankowski/*Francq*, Art. 34 para. 15.

as such irrelevant.[106] Consideration of these aspects would amount to a prohibited review of the judgment as to its substance. Moreover, only the result of the enforcement, not the judgment itself, must be considered.[107] Art. 34(1) has a residual role, i.e. it can only be invoked when the conditions of other defences – like Art. 34(2) and Art. 34(3) – are not met (*lex specialis derogate legi generali*).[108] Furthermore, a case concerning jurisdiction cannot be addressed under this provision because Art. 35 is exhaustively devoted to this defence.[109]

For practical reasons civil law commentators usually distinguish between procedural and substantive *ordre public*.[110] For the former the foreign procedure leading to the judgment must manifestly contradict with fundamental procedure law principles of the enforcement state, as was the case in *Krombach*.[111] The substantive *ordre public* requires the effects of the foreign judgment to be manifestly contrary to the fundamental principles of the legal order of the enforcement state.[112]

A special issue under Art. 34(1) is that of procedural fraud in the state of origin, for example, a claimant provided forged evidence. The *Schlosser Report* states such a case may come within the *ordre public* defence but means of redress in that State must be considered.[113] The English courts are even stricter. In addition to exhausting available remedies, the defendant must provide new evidence unavailable or unexamined in the original proceedings, and this evidence must have emerged too late to be raised on appeal in that State.[114] Even then the English court will normally not challenge the foreign judgment.[115] The *German Federal Court of Justice* is less strict and held it suffices that the debtor did not

---

[106] Case C-7/98 *Krombach v Bamberski* [2000] ECR I-1935, para. 36; cf. *L Cheshire/North/Fawcett*, Private International Law, p. 615.
[107] Jenard Report [1979] OJ C 59/1, p. 44; *Layton/Mercer*, EU Civil Practice I, para. 26.015.
[108] Case 145/86 *Hoffmann v Krieg* [1988] ECR I-645, para. 21; Case C-78/95 *Hendrikman v Magenta Druck & Verlag GmbH* [1996] ECR I-4943, para. 23.
[109] Case C-7/98 *Krombach v Bamberski* [2000] ECR I-1935, para.31.
[110] Cf. *Hess/Pfeiffer/Schlosser*, Heidelberg Report, para. 491; Magnus/Mankowski/*Francq*, Art. 34 paras. 20,28.
[111] Cf. Rauscher/*Leible*, Art. 34 Brüssel I-VO para. 13; *Hess*, Europäisches Zivilprozessrecht, p. 346; *Becker*, Grundrechtsschutz, p. 125.
[112] Cf. BGH (German Federal Court of Justice) NJW 1991, 1410; Rauscher/*Leible*, Art. 34 Brüssel I-VO para. 20.
[113] Schlosser Report [1979] OJ C 59/71, p. 128.
[114] *Interdesco SA v Nullifire Limited* [1992] I.L.Pr. 97, para. 35; cf. *Cheshire/North/Fawcett*, Private International Law, p. 613.
[115] Ibid. para. 38.

submit to the original proceedings, regardless of available means of redress.[116] However, this shifts the procedural burden to the enforcement state and gives the defendant a *second* chance of defence.[117] It is also contrary to the exceptional nature of the review under Art. 34 and 35 which requires the defendant to primarily argue his case and seek redress in the Member State of origin; expressly provided at the end of Art. 34(2). The discussion[118] whether fraud concerns the procedural or substantive *ordre public* is avoided by Common law lawyers by not adopting this categorisation. At any rate, the application must come within the limits set by the ECJ.

2. Art. 46 Commission Proposal

Art. 46 Proposal provides for a special judicial procedure before a court of the *Member State of enforcement* in which a party may seek a refusal of enforcement of the judgment on the ground that it "would not be permitted by the fundamental principles underlying the *right to a fair trial*." According to recital 24 Proposal this is to be understood as referring to all guarantees flowing from Art. 47 of the Charter of Fundamental Rights of the European Union[119] ('the Charter'). Arguably this includes the case-law of the European Court of Human Rights ('ECtHR') interpreting the corresponding Art. 6 ECHR.[120] Hence, enforcement can only be refused (Art. 46(5) Proposal) based on a breach of procedural guarantees afforded by *European fundamental rights law*. The fact that the Charter is not binding for the UK and Poland[121] should not be problematic since Art. 47 of the Charter is not directly concerned but only referred to for the interpretation of the directly binding Art. 46(1) Proposal.

3. Discussion

Art. 46(1) Proposal considerably limits the review standard compared to the *ordre public* defence in Art. 34(1) Brussels I. However, in the light of the final objective of free movement of judgments in the EU, one must ask first, whether

---

[116] BGH (German Federal Court of Justice) NJW 2004, 2388.

[117] Rauscher/*Leible*, Art. 34 Brüssel I-VO para. 18a; *Hess*, Europäisches Zivilprozessrecht, p. 349; *Georganti*, Ordre public, p. 105.

[118] The majority favours the procedural *ordre public*: Rauscher/*Leible*, Art. 34 Brüssel I-VO para. 18a; *Kropholler*, Art. 34 EuGVO para. 15b; for substantive *ordre public*: Magnus/Mankowski/*Francq*, Art. 34 para. 27.

[119] Charter on Fundamental Rights of the European Union [2000] OJ C 364/1.

[120] Cf. *Cuniberti/Rueda*, RabelsZ 2011, p. 313.

[121] Art.1(1) Protocol (No 30) on the application of the Charter of Fundamental Rights of the European Union to Poland and to the United Kingdom [2010] OJ C 83/313.

such a review is necessary at all, i.e. whether the Commission should have and could have gone further and entirely abolish the *ordre public* defence. This will be discussed from a fundamental rights perspective and a policy perspective. Then the particular limitations to the review standard proposed by Art. 46 Proposal will be critically discussed.

a) Abolishment of the ordre public defence - fundamental rights concerns

Under Brussels I the *ordre public* defence is often raised but seldom successful[122] which justifies asking: why not abolish this residual review all together? Indeed, this was already discussed prior to the Proposal in relation to the abolishment of the exequatur. This demonstrates that some commentators do not clearly distinguish both questions.[123] However, their perception may be influenced by some of the earlier regulations which abolished the exequatur in connection with the *ordre public* defence.[124] Moreover, the Green Paper of 2009 basically presents the abolition of the defences as a consequence of abolishing the exequatur.[125] This should not come as a surprise. Although, the Tampere Conclusion 1999 only mentioned the "further reduction of intermediate measures",[126] i.e. the exequatur procedure, the implementing 2000 Programme already proposed "limiting the reasons which can be given for challenging [...] enforcement of a foreign judgment ([e.g.], removal of the test of public policy, [...])", and in the long run, "abolition [...] of any checks on the judgment by courts in the requested country".[127] Thus, ultimately, the Commission plans to abolish all defences in the enforcement state to achieve full equal treatment of judgments given in the EU. However, it is necessary to analyse whether the prohibition of an *ordre public* review would comply with fundamental rights.

---

[122] *Hess/Pfeiffer/Schlosser*, Heidelberg Report, para. 481; Magnus/Mankowski/*Francq*, Art. 34 para.33.

[123] Cf. inter alia *Beaumont/Johnston*, J.Priv.Int.L. 2010, p. 270 et seq.; *Cuniberti/Rueda*, RabelsZ 2011, p. 304.

[124] Cf. Regulation 805/2004, Regulation 1896/2006, Regulation 861/2007.

[125] The Green Paper, COM(2009) 175 final, p. 3 see "Question 1".

[126] European Council, Tampere Conclusions 1999, para. 34.

[127] Council of the European Union, Draft programme of measures for implementation of the principle of mutual recognition of decisions in civil and commercial matters (11.2000) (hereinafter '2000 Programme'), OJ 2001 C 12/01, p. 5.

(1) The framework of human rights protection in the EU

Art. 6 TEU sets out three dimensions of European fundamental rights law. First, Art. 6(3) TEU codifies the case law of the ECJ establishing fundamental rights as part of the general principles of European law interpreted in the light of the common constitutional traditions and the ECHR.[128] Secondly, with the Treaty of Lisbon the Charter has become legally binding, Art. 6(1) TEU. The minimum standard of protection afforded by the Charter is defined by the ECHR.[129] Finally, Art. 6(2) TEU provides for the EU to accede to the ECHR which it has not done yet. However, it was already pointed out the ECHR indirectly already influences the fundamental rights protection at European level. Nonetheless, currently only the Member States are bound by the ECHR and the European institutions only have to comply (directly) with the European fundamental rights of the Charter and general principles of European law.

(2) The fundamental rights issues

Currently, if a judgment is given in breach of fundamental rights (in particular the right to a fair trial) its enforcement– or more specifically, the exequatur – can and shall be refused under Art. 34(1) Brussels I.[130] Therefore the abolishment of the *ordre public* defence would allow for the enforcement of judgments which are contrary to fundamental rights. It may put the enforcing state in conflict with its obligations under the ECHR. This conflict could be affected by the fact that EU secondary legislation would prohibit the Member States to refuse enforcement on this ground. Finally, it is questionable whether a regulation abolishing an *ordre public* review would comply with the fundamental rights in the Charter and the general principles of European law.

(3) The ECHR and enforcement without an ordre public review

(a) Art. 6 ECHR

In terms of a judgment being in breach of a fundamental right, the discussion most commonly centres on the right to a fair trial provided by Art. 6 ECHR. Art. 6(1) ECHR expressly provides the right "to a fair and public hearing within reasonable time by an independent and impartial tribunal established by law." The ECtHR clarified Art. 6(1) ECHR also guarantees the right of access to the courts

---

128 Cf. Case 4/73 *Nold v Commission* [1974] ECR I-491.
129 Art. 52(3), 53 of the Charter.
130 Case C-7/98 *Krombach v Bamberski* [2000] ECR I-1935, paras. 37 et seqq.

so that a denial may amount to a violation.[131] An analysis of the precise protection afforded under this provision to individuals is beyond the scope of this paper and unnecessary.[132] Instead, a judgment given in breach of Art. 6 ECHR is the prerequisite of the discussion. The issue of an abolished *ordre public* review is not about a (direct) violation of the right of access to a court by the enforcement state in respect of the creditor's original claim. He was already granted access to argue his civil claim by the court of origin and Art. 6 ECHR does not guarantee an appeal.[133] The question is whether Art. 6 ECHR has indirect effect so that the enforcement of the violating judgment without the possibility of a review constitutes a violation in itself.

(b) The indirect effects doctrine: Soering, Drozd and Pellegrini

In *Soering v United Kingdom,* the ECtHR first held that a State may violate Art. 6 ECHR by ordering a person to be extradited or deported to a country, whether or not a Convention State, where he runs a real risk of suffering treatment contrary to those provisions.[134] Hence, Art. 6 ECHR has indirect effect. The Contracting State is liable for facilitating the denial of the defendant's rights in another State's territory. This is the first example of the indirect effect of Art. 6 ECHR given by Judge *Matscher* in *Drozd and Janousek v France and Spain.*[135] He adds a Contracting State may also "incur responsibility by reason of assisting in the enforcement of a foreign judgment, originating from a Contracting State or a non-Contracting State, which has been obtained in [...] breach of Art. 6".

The leading case on the indirect effect of Art. 6 ECHR and the enforcement of foreign judgments, however, is *Pellegrini v Italy.*[136] In this case the ECtHR examined whether the Italian courts, before authorising enforcement of the Vatican court decision annulling the applicant's marriage, duly satisfied themselves that the relevant proceedings fulfilled the guarantees of Art. 6.[137] Hence, Art. 6 ECHR creates a duty to enforce only foreign judgments which comply with the

---

[131] *Golder v United Kingdom*, No. 4451/70 (1975) 1 EHRR 524, para. 36.

[132] For a full analysis cf. *Harris/O'Boyle/Warbrick*, ECHR, p. 201; Frowein/Peukert/*Peukert*, Art. 6 EMRK.

[133] *Delcourt v Belgium*, No. 2689/65 (1970) 1 EHRR 255, para. 25; also *Stein*, IPRax 2004, p. 186.

[134] *Soering v United Kingdom*, No. 14038/88 (1992) 14 EHRR 745, paras. 91, 113.

[135] Drozd and Janousek v France and Spain, No. 12747/87 (1992) 14 EHRR 745.

[136] *Pellegrini v Italy*, No. 30882/96 (2001) 35 EHRR 44.

[137] Ibid. para. 40.

ECHR.[138] Though, it was also stated that "a review of that kind is required where a decision [...] emanates from the courts of a country which does not apply the Convention." This remark causes uncertainty whether *Pellegrini* also applies to judgments given in a Contracting State. No such case has been decided by the ECtHR yet. In case of affirmation, the Member States would be obliged to conduct a fundamental rights review before the enforcement.

In *Government of the United States of America v Montgomery (No 2),* the House of Lords held that *Pellegrini* had to be confined to its facts as it turned on the special relationship between the Italian civil court and the Vatican court based on the Concordant, and thus is not a general authority.[139] This has been criticized arguing that the relevant statement of law by the ECtHR – cited above – does not refer to this relationship but is rather general.[140] Interestingly, *Lord Carswell* after distinguishing *Pellegrini* endorses obiter the indirect effect of Art. 6 ECHR in enforcement cases regardless of the origin of the judgment.[141] However, the wording of the ECtHR concluding remark suggests (*e contrario*) a limitation to judgments from non-Contracting States. It is also argued that if the judgment is given in a Contracting State the possible individual application under Art. 34 ECHR against that state provides sufficient protection.[142] The victim does not need the option to raise the violation in another state. For the enforcement this would mean in a presumption that judgments from other Contracting States comply with Art. 6 ECHR.

It is, however, not clear why the fact that the state of origin is itself bound by the ECHR should release the enforcing state from its responsibility as a Contracting State. The latter would have to enforce even obviously violating judgments. Moreover, it seems odd that in one case the enforcement shall carry with it an independent fundamental rights responsibility but not in the other, although both cases may concern the same European citizen. Hence, the enforcement without review is not a mere perpetuation of the original violation but a new breach of Art. 6 ECHR.[143] The suggested presumption appears unjustified against the background of several cases in which the ECtHR found Member

---

[138] cf. *Cuniberti*, ICLQ 2008, p. 30.
[139] [2004] 1 WLR 2241, para. 21.
[140] *Fawcett*, ICLQ 2007, p. 35; *Briggs*, BYBIL 2004, p. 541; *Cuniberti*, ICLQ 2008, p. 30.
[141] Government of the United States of America v Montgomery (No 2) [2004] 1 WLR 2241, paras. 24, 27.
[142] *Kinsch* in Einhorn/Siehr, Essays in Memory of Nygh,p. 228; *Stein*, IPRax 2004, p. 187.
[143] *Rauscher*, Europäischer Vollstreckungstitel, p. 14; *Kohler* in Reichelt/Rechberger (ed.), Europäisches Kollisionsrecht, p. 77.

States in violation of Art. 6 ECHR.[144] *Cuniberti* rightly argues judgments from Contracting States in breach of Art. 6 ECHR should have even less chance to be enforced (*a fortiori*).[145] Finally, the distinction seems inconsistent with the prior case law, which did not distinguish between Contracting and non-Contracting States, although, the possibility of an individual application in the other state could have been argued as well. It is therefore submitted that the Contracting States are generally obliged by the ECHR to deny enforcement of judgments in breach of Art. 6 ECHR, i.e. conduct a prior fundamental rights review.[146]

Finally, it should be noted that the obligation to conduct a review before enforcement does not conflict with a preclusion rule in case remedies in the state of origin are not exhausted, or a rule that the review is not conducted *ex officio*. In both scenarios the individual is given the opportunity to receive protection before the enforcement. Not taking advantage of it can be regarded as a waiver of the protection provided by the fundamental right. Thus it releases the Contracting State from its obligation.[147]

(c) Enforcement implementing an obligation of European law

Having identified an obligation under Art. 6 ECHR to review foreign judgments before enforcement, it is necessary to consider the fact that the Member States would be prohibited from conducting such a review by a European regulation. The conflict may be solved by a provision giving preference to the ECHR. Art. 71 Brussels I and the identical Art. 82 Proposal give preference to conventions which govern the recognition or enforcement of judgments in relation to particular matters. Art. 6 ECHR imposes obligations in relation to enforcement but, unlike the example conventions listed in the *Schlosser Report,*[148] it is not confined to particular matters. Commentators on Art. 71 Brussels I also make no

---

[144] *Cf. Krombach v France*, No. 29731/96 (2001) 12 HR Case Digest 76; *Cuniberti/Rueda*, RabelsZ 2011, p. 296.

[145] *Cuniberti*, ICLQ 2008, p. 31; *Schilling*, IPRax 2011, p. 34; *Thoma*, Europäisierung des ordre public, p. 102.

[146] Like this *Cuniberti/Rueda*, RabelsZ 2011, p. 299; *Harris/O'Boyle/Warbrick*, ECHR, p. 203; *Matscher* in FS für Kollhosser II, p. 438; *Rechberger* in FS für Leipold, p. 307; arguable according to *Fawcett*, ICLQ 2007, p. 5.

[147] For the admissibility of a waiver cf. *Pauger v Austria*, No. 16717/90 (1997) 25 EHRR 105, para.58.

[148] Schlosser Report [1979] OJ C 59/71, p. 150 (fn.59).

reference to the ECHR.[149] Hence, in principle, there is a conflict of obligations for the Member States.

From the perspective of the ECHR the starting point for solving this conflict must be the case-law of the ECtHR. In order to reconcile the legitimate interest of international cooperation and the function of the ECHR, the ECtHR held in *Bosphorus Airways v Ireland* that there is a presumption of compliance with the ECHR of acts by the Contracting State which implement a strict – not discretionary – obligation flowing from its membership in an international organization so long as this organisation provides human rights protection that is equivalent – not identical – to that in the Convention.[150] This test is reminiscent to the *Solange-II* doctrine of the German Constitutional Court.[151] With reference to the reliance on the ECHR as a source of human rights protection in European law (now Art. 6(3) TEU), and to the remedies provided to the ECJ the protection afforded by the EU was held equivalent in terms of substance and mechanisms.[152] Under the Treaty of Lisbon there has not been a change of these aspects justifying a different conclusion. An obligation of direct enforcement, i.e. prohibition of a review, would be strict, leaving no room for discretion so that the *Bosphorus* presumption would apply. However, the presumption can be rebutted if, in the particular case, the protection provided is 'manifestly deficient'. This case-by-case assessment of the protection provided differs to the purely abstract comparison by the German Constitutional Court under *Solange-II*. In *Bosphorus* a rebuttal was rejected with rather general reference to the nature of the interference, the general interest pursued by the act and a preliminary ruling. Hence, the 'manifest deficiency test' appears to be a high hurdle which explains why, in this context, such a case has not yet been found to exist.[153] Arguably this would be the same in the present case. The free movement of judgments within the EU is certainly a legitimate aim. The level of fundamental rights protection in the EU is at least such, as provided by the ECHR, and just as in *Bosphorus*

---

[149] Cf. Magnus/Mankowski/*Mankowski*, Art. 71 para. 9, Rauscher/*Mankowski*, Art. 71 Brüssel I-VO para. 6.

[150] Bosphorus Hava Yollari Turizm ve Ticaret Anonim Sirketi v Ireland, No.45036/98(2005) 42 EHRR 1,155-157.

[151] The *Solange* doctrine requires that the standards of protection of fundamental rights in the EU be *generally* lower for the presumption of equivalence to the German fundamental rights protection to be rebutted. *cf.* BVerfGE 73, 339, *Re the application of Wünsche Handelsgesellschaft (Solange II)* [1987] 3 C.M.L.R. 225.

[152] Ibid. paras. 159-165. Even the only indirect individual benefit of a request for a preliminary ruling by a national court according to Art. 267 TFEU was held to be sufficient.

[153] Cf. *Lock*, HRLRev 2010, p. 545 and the case-law cited.

the validity of the regulation could be reviewed *inter alia* in proceedings for a preliminary ruling (Art. 267 TFEU). In case a regulation provides less protection of the right to a fair trial it will be invalid for being in breach of European fundamental rights as primary European law. Thus, Member States which enforce a foreign judgment without prior review acting in accordance with a *valid* European regulation obliging them, would not breach the ECHR. However, the crucial question is whether such a regulation would actually be valid.

(4) Fundamental rights and legality of a Regulation without any review

A regulation is part of secondary European law and thus, to be valid, has to comply with superior primary European law of which the European fundamental rights form an integral part, Art. 6 TEU. It has been demonstrated above that Art. 6 ECHR defines the minimum level of protection under Art. 47 of the Charter and the European general principles. Therefore, it can be concluded that the European right to a fair trial also requires a review of the foreign judgment before its enforcement. However, it is submitted that a review either in the Member State of origin or the Member State of enforcement is sufficient. This does not contradict the above finding in respect to the ECHR. In this relation the enforcing Contracting State is entirely sovereign and autonomously decides to conduct no prior review. It seems to be this very autonomy in relation to the ECHR which justifies the independent responsibility under Art. 6 ECHR (indirect effect). The situation is different in the scenario relating to European fundamental rights, although most commentators do not seem to clearly distinguish both relationships. The EU Member States limited their sovereignty in the area of cross-border enforcement of European judgments by providing the EU with competences in this area. A regulation prohibiting an *ordre public* review before enforcement would be a strict act of harmonisation. It would leave the Member States no discretion, the exercise of which would require them to comply with European fundamental rights. Hence, the European fundamental rights responsibility is concentrated with the regulation. As long as there is no harmonisation of the civil procedure rules of the Member States the regulation must provide for legal protection of the right to a fair trial with a possible review. From the European perspective, however, it seems sufficient that effective legal protection is provided at all.[154] It should not be relevant whether this is in the origin or the enforcement Member State. As seen above, mutual trust can be demanded from

---

[154] Like this *Bach*, Grenzüberschreitende Vollstreckung, p. 384; *Schilling*, IPRax 2011, p. 35.

the Member States. Ultimately, this resembles the line of thinking adopted by the ECtHR in *Bosphorus*. Whether shifting the review to the Member State of origin would be the ideal solution is a different question to be decided on policy grounds.[155] At any rate, a regulation which prohibits any review of the foreign judgment as to its compliance with European fundamental rights would arguably be invalid,[156] i.e. a review must either be allowed under national remedies or the regulation must provide a special remedy.

(5) Individual application to the ECtHR - a sufficient remedy?

It is argued against the submitted obligation that the victim of a breach of the right to a fair trial can always lodge an individual application (Art. 34 ECHR) to the ECHR against the respective Member State. This shall suffice as protection and make a review by a national court dispensable.[157] However, concerns are justified for theoretical and practical reasons. First and foremost, the ECtHR has no power to cancel a judgment given in breach of fundamental rights. It will thus remain and continue to produce effects. Furthermore, an individual application does not prevent the enforcement of the judgment in breach.[158] The ECtHR can only find a breach of the applicant's rights and afford just satisfaction, i.e. damages.[159] Moreover, because of the necessary exhaustion of all domestic remedies (Art. 35 ECHR) together with usually long-lasting proceedings before the ECtHR, legal protection would regularly come too late to be really effective.[160] The individual application would only be a sufficient remedy if the regulation provided that lodging it could suspend the enforcement, and that the finding of the ECtHR is binding.

---

[155] For this discussion cf. infra p. 35.

[156] Several commentators argue that Regulation 805/2004 and the other regulations which abolished the *ordre public* review are invalid, *Cuniberti*, ICLQ 2008, p. 50; *Rauscher*, Europäischer Vollstreckungstitel, p. 15; *Kohler* in Reichelt/Rechberger (ed.), Europäisches Kollisionsrecht, p. 77 et seq. Therefore the recent ECJ decision Case C-491/10 *Joseba Andoni Aguirre Zarraga v Simone Pelz* (yet unreported in the ECR) must at least be criticised for not addressing the lack of a fundamental rights review under Regulation 2201/2003.

[157] *Bach*, Grenzüberschreitende Vollstreckung, p. 384.

[158] Cf. *Georganti*, Ordre public, p. 120.

[159] Art. 41 ECHR, cf. *Cuniberti/Rueda*, RabelsZ 2011, p. 295; *Georganti*, Ordre public, p. 121.

[160] *Hess*, Europäisches Zivilprozessrecht, p. 552; For statistics on cases pending before the ECtHR cf. http://www.echr.coe.int/ECHR/EN/Header/Reports+and+Statistics/Statistics/Statistical+information+by+year/ (last accessed: 07.08.2011).

However, there is a serious practical argument against relying solely on the ECtHR. *Cuniberti* and *Rueda* signify a recent reluctance of the ECtHR to get involved in certain cases. Applications were held "inadmissible for being manifestly ill-founded when the case [...] seemed very serious indeed."[161] The best example is the *Gambazzi* case which came before the ECJ and the ECtHR.[162] Gambazzi was a defendant in English fraud proceedings who refused to fully comply with the several interim orders addressed to him by the court. As a consequence he was debarred from defending, even on the merits of the case, and hence lost automatically. The Italian court, which was requested to recognize the English default judgments, referred the case to the ECJ under Art. 267 TFEU in asking whether the *ordre public* clause of the former Art. 27(1) Brussels Convention must be applied because of a violation of the defendant's right to be heard. Although the ECJ gave no final answer on the question of fact, it provided sufficient guidance for the national court by holding that Gambazzi had suffered "the most serious restriction possible on the rights of the defence", and that such a restriction "must satisfy very exacting requirements if it is not to be regarded as a manifest and disproportionate infringement of those rights."[163] Whereas the ECJ obviously found the case to be very serious, the ECtHR rejected Gambazzi's application as manifestly ill-founded. This is strong evidence that the EU should not exclusively rely on the ECtHR for the protection of fundamental rights.

(6) Interim conclusion

The analysis of the obligations arising from fundamental rights – especially the right to a fair trial – for Member States and for the validity of a European regulation revealed that there is still much discussion and uncertainty involved as to the requirements for sufficient protection. It is submitted that an European regulation, in order to be valid, must allow for a fundamental rights review of the foreign judgment[164] either in the origin or the enforcement Member State. In the former case the Member State of enforcement refraining from the review in compliance with the regulation would not violate Art. 6 ECHR under *Bosphorus*. Hence, from a fundamental rights perspective it is possible to avoid this intermediate procedure in the Member State of enforcement, although this is not to

---

[161] Cf. *Cuniberti/Rueda*, RabelsZ 2011, p. 295.

[162] Case C-394/07 *Gambazzi v DaimlerCrysler Canada* [2009] ECR I-2569.

[163] Ibid. para. 33; cf. Also the case comment by *Cuniberti*, IPRax 2010, p. 152.

[164] Like this *Cuniberti*, ICLQ 2008, p. 50; Beaumont/Johnston, J.Priv.Int.L. 2010, p. 273; *Rauscher*, Europäischer Vollstreckungstitel, p. 15; *Kohler* in Reichelt/Rechberger (ed.), Europäisches Kollisionsrecht, p. 77.

argue that this would indeed be the ideal solution. The regulation may allow a review according to the national laws or provide for a special (harmonised) remedy as envisaged by the Proposal. The review may be conditional to the initiative of a party and the exhaustion of available remedies. In any case, the EU should not rely solely on the individual application to the ECtHR under Art. 34 ECHR. However, there are admittedly also commentators arguing that such a review by a Member State court is unnecessary[165] and this may infer support from the several special regulations which abolished the *ordre public* review.[166]

b) The continuing need for an ordre public review

Even if European fundamental rights would not require a review prior to the enforcement, it may still be appropriate to maintain an *ordre public* review. At first this may seem implausible. The survey conducted for the *Heidelberg Report* provided that the *ordre public* defence, although often raised, is generally refused.[167] There seems to be no need to uphold such a strong obstacle to the free movement of judgments to provide protection which is hardly ever required. The *ordre public* review is regarded as an 'emergency-break' or 'the last bastion' for the protection of fundamental principles and moral concepts of each Member State.[168] As such, its existence expresses mutual distrust and contradicts the Commission's basis for facilitating the free movement of judgments in the EU. On the other hand, the small number of successful cases could equally be taken as evidence that the *ordre public* defence is not a real obstacle. Reliance on it for the sole purpose of causing a delay can be addressed by simply putting the cost burden on the unsuccessful defendant, as provided by Art. 46(8) Proposal. More importantly, however, it has been demonstrated that the protection of fundamental rights forms an integral part of the *ordre public* defence. Although it is not doubted that the Member States' legal systems are generally characterised by the protection of human rights and the rule of law,[169] the case

---

[165] Cf. *Wagner*, IPRax 2002, p. 87; *Stein*, IPRax 2004, p. 187; *Bach*, Grenzüberschreitende Vollstreckung, p. 388

[166] Cf. Regulations 805/2004, 1896/2006, 861/2007 but Art. 24 Regulation 4/2009 contains an *ordre public* clause again.

[167] *Hess/Pfeiffer/Schlosser*, Heidelberg Report, para. 481; also Magnus/Mankowski/*Francq*, Art. 34 para. 33.

[168] Cf. *Leible*, ecolex 2011, p. 709; *Georganti*, Ordre Public, p. 145; *Oberhammer*, IPRax 2010, p. 201.

[169] Cf. Rauscher/*Leible*, Art. 34 Brüssel I-VO para. 13; *Georganti*, Ordre public, p. 138.

law over the last years shows there are still exceptional circumstances, in which this defence is needed in order to adequately protect those rights.[170]

In *Krombach,* the German Federal Court of Justice refused the exequatur for a French judgment for civil damages based on a criminal offence using the *ordre public* defence, after the ECJ had provided its important interpretation thereof.[171] Since the defendant refused to appear in person, although he was duly summoned to do so, he was found in contempt of court and thus denied representation by a lawyer. That was a clear violation of every defendant's right of defence, particularly the right to be heard, and thus of elementary notions of a fair trial.[172]

The Court of Appeal in *Maronier v Larmer*[173] refused to grant the exequatur for a Dutch judgment relying on the *ordre public* defence. He held that the defendant had manifestly not received a fair trial because he was unaware that Dutch proceedings against him, which had been stayed for twelve years, had been reactivated until after the time for an appeal in the Netherlands had passed. It should be noted, the Court of Appeal reached this decision although it applies a strong presumption that the procedure laws of all ECHR Contracting States comply with the right to a fair trial (Art. 6 ECHR).[174]

In another case, the German Federal Court of Justice denied recognition of a Polish maintenance judgment based solely upon hearsay evidence by the minor claimant's grandmother who cared for the child.[175] The German defendant contested that he had had any sexual intercourse with the mother, offered physical proof and requested a medical expert opinion regarding his paternity. This was ignored by the Polish court which, according to the German court, was a breach of the defendant's right to be heard.

Finally, one should recall the *Gambazzi* case where the defendant in English proceedings was debarred from defending the case for non-compliance with the

---

170 *Hess/Pfeiffer/Schlosser*, Heidelberg Report, para. 479.

171 BGH (German Federal Court of Justice) NJW 2000, 3289 after Case C-7/98 *Krombach v Bamberski* [2000] ECR I-1935.

172 Only indirectly the ECJ in Case C-7/98 *Krombach v Bamberski* [2000] ECR I-1935, paras. 40; directly *Beaumont/Johnston*, J.Priv.Int.L. 2010, p. 254; *Schack* in FS für Erecinski, forthcoming.

173 *Maronier v Lamer* [2003] QB 620, paras. 37 et seq.

174 Ibid. para. 25.

175 BGH (German Federal Court of Justice) NJW 2009, 3306 para. 31; see also *Schlosser*, IPRax 2010, p. 103.

several interim orders addressed to him by the court. Upon the request of the Italian court the ECJ clarified that, in principle, this represented "the most serious restriction possible on the rights of the defence".[176] Hence, the earlier exequatur decision of the French Court de cassation must be criticised for rejecting the *ordre public* defence on the grounds that the English proceedings were compliant with English civil procedure law.[177]

These cases demonstrate that the procedural laws of the Member States have not yet converged enough to abolish, at least, the procedural *ordre public* defence. Moreover, they confirm again that the continuously emphasised mutual trust is not sufficiently supported by the legal reality.[178] Nevertheless, the described cases resulted from the correct application of the respective national procedural laws. The subsequent amendment of the respective laws in compliance with European fundamental rights is taken as an argument that, by now, the defence has become superfluous.[179] This either suggests that all cases which could possibly trigger the defence have already arisen and resulted in such amendments, or (more realistic) that the rare success of the defence justifies its abolishment. However, the fact that cases like these are rare and become even rarer cannot justify the abolishment of a defence the whole purpose of which is to provide a safeguard for exceptional "catastrophic" cases.[180] It is because of their required severe impact that these cases are so exceptional. Cases like those presented above can only be prevented through harmonisation. For the time being there will be no such harmonisation so that the abolishment of the defence would sacrifice the seldom individuals who experienced gross injustice on the altar of mutual trust between the Member States.[181] Hence, the individual rights protection afforded by the *ordre public* should not give way to the postulate of mutual trust, i.e. human rights protection must prevail. The protection of domestic public interests and objective principles seems to be at least not of comparable importance.[182] The declining role of these aspects is already evidenced by the fact that their protection under Brussels I is conditional on the initiative of a

---

[176] Case C-394/07 *Gambazzi v DaimlerCrysler Canada* [2009] ECR I-2569, para. 33.

[177] Civ.1ére, 30 juin 2004,*Stolzenberg c. CIBC Mellon Trust*, IPRax 2006,p.300; cf. *Cuniberti*, IPRax 2010,p. 152.

[178] *Schlosser*, IPRax 2010, p. 104; *Schack* in FS für Erecinski, forthcoming; *Georganti*, Ordre public, p. 138.

[179] Cf. *Hess/Pfeiffer/Schlosser*, Heidelberg Report, p. 145 fn.748; *Schlosser*, IPRax 2010, p. 104.

[180] *Oberhammer*, JBl. 2006, p. 497.

[181] *Cuniberti/Rueda*, RabelsZ 2011, p. 304; *Kuipers*, CYELP 2010, p. 47.

[182] Like this Rauscher/*Pabst*, Art. 5 EG-VollstrTitelVO para. 12.

party appealing against the exequatur and raising the defence of Art. 34(1) because Art. 43(1) and Art. 45(1) Brussels I clearly contradict an assessment *ex officio.*[183]

The abolishment of the *ordre public* review would also dispose of a limitation generally accepted in the EU's core area of economic policy.[184] The European area of freedom, security and justice would, metaphorically speaking, rush ahead of those policies. The Treaty of Lisbon has not abolished the 'public policy' exception, which is based in particular on the *Cassis de Dijon*[185] formula, for the four freedoms.[186] Accordingly, on the basis of a lack of common rules and disparities between the national laws, some fundamental values are respected as limits on the free movement of goods, services, capital and people, even though, those values are not necessarily shared throughout the EU.[187] Of course, there is no general rule that the free movement of judgments could not be wider than the economic freedoms. However, if a public policy exception is accepted and regarded as necessary in this core area of European law because of disparities between the national laws, one must inevitably ask how such disparities shall suddenly be overcome on the basis of mutual trust to achieve free movement of judgments in the EU.

Finally, it may be added that even in the USA and Canada, which certainly form more integrated markets than the EU, courts of a state can refuse the enforcement of a judgment from another state on grounds similar to the *ordre public* defence.[188] It demonstrates that even more integrated markets obviously regard the 'emergency-break' of an *ordre public* defence as adequate and necessary.

It can be concluded, that even if there was no European fundamental rights obligation, there are convincing arguments to maintain the *ordre public* defence, at least, to the extent to which it affords protection for these rights. The presented case law demonstrated that the disparities between the Member States'

---

[183] Cf. *Georganti*, Ordre Public,p. 107; *Sujecki*, ZEuP 2008, p. 464.
[184] Cf. *inter alia Kuipers*, CYELP 2010, p. 49.
[185] Case 120/78 *Rewe-Zentral AG v Bundesmonopolverwaltung für Branntwein (Cassis de Dijon)* [1979] ECR I-649, para.8 accepting certain 'mandatory requirements' as non-written exceptions to the four freedoms.
[186] Cf. also Art. 36, 45(3), 53(1), 62, and 65(1)(b) TFEU.
[187] *Beaumont/Johnston*, J.Priv.Int.L. 2010, p. 277.
[188] *Lee v Winston*, 1983, 717 F.2d 888 (Va.); *Fraguela v Fraguela*, 1991, 576 N.Y.S.2d 669; *Castel/Walker*, Canadian Conflict of Laws, para. 14.24; *Schack* in FS für Erecinski, forthcoming; *Schlosser*, IPRax 2010,p. 102.

procedural laws, due to a lack of harmonisation, still give raise to exceptional cases of manifest violations. For the time being, the *ordre public* defence is still indispensable because fundamental rights protection must prevail over the postulate of mutual trust.

c) Harmonisation of minimum standards

Having identified the divergence especially of the procedural laws as a reason for maintaining, at least the procedural *ordre public*, one might argue in favour of introducing procedural minimum standards ensuring compliance with the right to a fair trial following the example of the other adopted regulations.[189] However, the minimum standards of these regulations are only concerned with the right of prior notice to protect the defendant's right of defence, i.e. only a part of the protection afforded under Art. 47 of the Charter (and Art. 6 ECHR).[190] In order to ensure full compliance with all guarantees of the right to a fair trial the minimum standard provisions would have to be quite elaborate taking into account the existing case law of the ECtHR,[191] and thus be extensive. Such a casuistic approach does not only seem impractical but, more importantly, would 'freeze' the protection provided by the regulation at the *status quo* of the case law. It would not allow the consideration of new developments, i.e. it would be inflexible. Therefore, it is submitted that the approach of minimum standards is impractical to ensure full compliance with Art. 47 ECHR rather than only with its arguably most important aspects. Hence, as long as the national procedure laws are not harmonised in compliance with Art. 47 ECHR, a general clause like Art. 46 Proposal allowing for a review is necessary. This general clause would always have to be interpreted in compliance with the current state of the fundamental rights case law. It must therefore be endorsed that the Commission's Proposal opted for a more general review in Art. 46(1) Proposal.

d) Art. 46 Proposal – A reduction to procedural ordre public

Art. 46(1) Proposal provides a remedy for violations of the right to a fair trial and accordingly reflects the prominent role of this right in the definition of the *ordre public* defence of Art. 34(1) Brussels I that is also demonstrated by the cases mentioned above. The right to a fair trial lies at the heart of the procedural

---

[189] Cf. Chapter III Regulation 805/2004; Art. 13-15 Regulation 1896/2006; Art. 13 Regulation 861/2007.

[190] Cf. *Oberhammer*, IPRax 2010, p. 201; *Cuniberti/Rueda*, RabelsZ 2011, p. 298.

[191] *Cuniberti/Rueda*, RabelsZ 2011, p. 300.

ordre public.[192] With Art. 46(1) Proposal the Commission thus obviously intends to abolish the substantive *ordre public.*[193] The Proposal states no reasons for this limitation. The Commission may put forward that, in practice, courts of Member States virtually never deny enforcement of judgments on the grounds of the substantive *ordre public.*[194] According to *Rauscher* its insignificant role is further evidenced by the fact that other commentators[195] have obvious problems to provide realistic example cases for its justification when they refer to claims from drug deals, gambling debts and the possible introduction of punitive damages.[196] The *Heidelberg Report* asserts that there are no fundamental differences between the Member States' legal systems in relation to civil and commercial matters which could trigger the application of the substantive *ordre public.*[197] This is a result of the increasing harmonisation of substantive laws and PIL rules of the Member States, especially the Rome I Regulation[198] and the Rome II Regulation.[199] Moreover, it is argued[200] that sufficient protection against critical substantive law is provided by the court of origin through the *ordre public* exception contained in Art. 21 Rome I and Art. 26 Rome II.

Nevertheless, it is submitted Art. 46 Proposal should be amended reintroducing the substantive *ordre public*. The right to a fair trial is indeed the most prominent fundamental right in the definition of *ordre public* but it is not clear why Art. 46 Proposal neglects all other fundamental rights which would be part of the substantive *ordre public.*[201] The important role of the *ordre public* clause for the protection of fundamental rights has been identified before and the

---

[192] *Meidanis*, ELRev 2005, p. 109.

[193] Endorsed by *Oberhammer*, IPRax 2010, p. 202; *Hess*, IPRax 2011, p. 128; *Rauscher*, Europäischer Vollstreckungstitel, p. 10.

[194] *Hess/Pfeiffer/Schlosser*, Heidelberg Report, para. 491; also *Cuniberti/Rueda*, RabelsZ 2011, p. 313.

[195] Cf. *Wagner*, IPRax 2002, p. 90 with further references.

[196] *Rauscher*, Europäischer Vollstreckungstitel, p. 10; cf. also *Heringer*, Europäischer Vollstreckungstitel, p. 83.

[197] *Hess/Pfeiffer/Schlosser*, Heidelberg Report, para. 491; also *Layton/Mercer*, EU Civil Practice I, para. 26.015.

[198] Regulation (EC) No 593/2008 of the European Parliament and of the Council of 17 June 2008 on the law applicable to contractual obligations [2008] OJ L 177/6 (hereinafter 'Rome I').

[199] Regulation (EC) No 864/2007 of the European Parliament and of the Council of 11 July 2007 on the law applicable to non-contractual obligations [2007] OJ L 199/40 (hereinafter 'Rome II').

[200] *Hess*, IPRax 2011, p. 129; *Schack* in FS für Ericinski, forthcoming.

[201] *Cuniberti/Rueda*, RabelsZ 2011, p. 313; European Parliament, Draft Report of 26 June 2011 (2010/0383(COD)), p. 46.

Commission can hardly believe that compliance with the right to a fair trial is more important than compliance with other fundamental rights. The limitation must therefore relate to practical relevance. However, it has already been argued for the *ordre public* in general; the mere fact of very rare cases in the past and a decreasing probability resulting from increased harmonisation cannot serve as a basis to abolish a defence, the purpose of which is to provide a safeguard for exceptional cases.

Art. 46(1) Proposal not only excludes all other fundamental rights but also the economic freedoms and the rules on European Competition Law (Art. 101 et seqq TFEU) which are considered part of the (substantive) European *ordre public* under Art. 34(1) Brussels I.[202] Moreover, it is argued that the EU may agree on certain clear political objectives in its treatment of a particular state.[203] The enforcement of a judgment undermining these objectives could not be prevented with such a fair trial defence.

Even the *Heidelberg Report* adds to the statement above, "it cannot be excluded that a substantive *ordre public* exception will still be needed in unavoidable and extreme situations" and therefore this exception should be maintained.[204] The final decision in *Volker Sonntag*[205] serves as evidence for such a rare case. The German Federal Court of Justice refused to recognise and enforce an Italian judgment because it was held contrary to the German *ordre public* (under Art. 27(1) Brussels Convention). The Italian court had ordered a German teacher personally to pay damages to the parents of a German schoolboy who had been the victim of a fatal accident during an excursion to Italy. However, under German law the teacher was exempted from such claims which were included in the statutory accident insurance scheme.[206] The exemption from civil claims was essential because under the scheme the injured person was entitled to flat-rate compensation. Enforcing the Italian judgment would have undermined the basis of the social accident insurance scheme, which ensures a balance of the

---

[202] Case C-38/98 *Régie Nationale Des Usines Renault Sa v Maxicar SpA and Orazio Formento* [2000] ECR I-2973, para.32 although ultimately the ECJ did not find a 'manifest breach'; Case C-128/97 *Eco Swiss China Time v Benetton International* [1999] ECR-3055, paras. 39, 41; cf. *Meidanis*, ELRev 2005, p. 105.

[203] *Beaumont/Johnston*, J.Priv.Int.L. 2010, p. 259.

[204] *Hess/Pfeiffer/Schlosser*, Heidelberg Report, para. 491 and 557.

[205] BGH (German Federal Court of Justice) IPRax 1994, 118. The judgment was strongly criticised for finding a 'manifest breach', cf. *Bach*, Grenzüberschreitende Vollstreckung, p. 468 et seq.; *Hess*, Europäisches Zivilprozessrecht, p. 348.

[206] Formerly: §§ 636, 637, 548, 539(1) Nr.14(b) RVO (Reichsversicherungsordnung), Today: §§ 104, 105, 8, 2(1) Nr.8(b) SGB VII (Sozialgesetzbuch VII).

involved interests by the transfer of liability from the injuring party to the provider of the insurance.[207] The Member State laws are not yet harmonised to an extent rendering such cases impossible.[208]

Yet even if they had been, according to Rome I and Rome II the applicable law may be that of a third country (Art. 2 Rome I and Art. 3 Rome II), i.e. a Member State court's judgment could still be based on non-harmonised rules. The protection afforded by the PIL *ordre public* clauses of Art. 21 Rome I and Art. 26 Rome II is insufficient. Both provisions only allow for the consideration of the *ordre public* of the forum, i.e. the protection afforded at the PIL level varies. This shortcoming is even aggravated by the possibility of 'forum shopping' under the jurisdiction rules of Brussels I and the Proposal. Moreover, it seems inconsistent that a court applying another law could rely on the *ordre public* of its forum under Rome I and Rome II, but could not reject the enforcement of a judgment based on the same law.[209] Hence, the current state of harmonisation of the substantive laws and PIL within the EU does not allow for the abolishment of the substantive *ordre public*.[210]

Finally, it is at least questionable whether the fair trial defence of Art. 46(1) Proposal covers the practically most relevant[211] case in which the foreign judgment is obtained by (procedural) fraud.[212] The question arises regardless of the characterisation as part of the substantive or procedural *ordre public*. Doubts are justified because the right to a fair trial provides procedural guarantees to be obeyed by the court to protect the defendant. These doubts do not seem diminished if a court, having exhausted its procedural possibilities, simply bases its decision on false facts, for example, because of forged evidence. Indeed, this suggests that the concept of procedural *ordre public* is wider than the right to a fair trial which is support by the fact that fraud and the right to a fair trial are generally discussed independently under this topic.[213] In order to protect the de-

---

[207] Cf. *Beaumont/Johnston*, J.Priv.Int.L. 2010, p. 262; *Hess/Pfeiffer/Schlosser*, Heidelberg Report, para. 480.

[208] Like this *inter alia Leible*, ecolex 2011, p. 709.

[209] European Parliament, Draft Report of 26 June 2011 (2010/0383(COD)), p. 46; *Leible*, ecolex 2011, p. 709.

[210] Like this *Beaumont/Johnston*, J.Priv.Int.L. 2010, p. 264; *Hess/Pfeiffer/Schlosser*, Heidelberg Report, para. 557; *Leible*, ecolex 2011, p. 709; arguably also *Cuniberty/Rueda*, RabelsZ 2011, p. 313.

[211] *Hess/Pfeiffer/Schlosser*, Heidelberg Report, para. 492.

[212] *Hess*, IPRax 2011, p. 129 regards this situation as covered without stating any reasons.

[213] Cf. *Cheshire/North/Fawcett*, Private International Law, p. 612 et seqq.; *Dicey/Morris/Collins*, Conflict of Laws I, para. 14-209.

fendant, enforcement of judgments obtained by fraud should also be covered by the new defence, albeit, with the caution expressed in the *Schlosser Report*.[214] In the light of the different approaches adopted by Member State courts, a more detailed provision or explanatory notes in the recitals would be welcomed.

e) Denationalisation – The standard of Art. 47 of the Charter

With its reference to Art. 47 of the Charter, recital 24 of the Proposal stipulates that Art. 46(1) Proposal establishes a European standard of protection. This would be another fundamental change to the national concept of Art. 34(1) Brussels I. Such Europeanization implicates that the ECJ will be able to determine the content rather than merely the limits of the concept. The ECJ decisions in *Krombach*, *Eco Swiss v Benetton* and *Renault v Maxicar* already allowed for the identification of a 'European *ordre public*' as part of the Member State's *ordre public*.[215] It has to be observed by the national courts and may add or correct aspects of the national concept.[216] For the Commission it is obviously time to rely solely on a supranational concept. Indeed, one must ask whether, in a single European area of justice, national values and principles should still be given effect.[217] However, Art. 67(1) TFEU also demands respect for the different legal systems and traditions of the Member States. The latter would risk internal conflicts, especially through enforcement of judgments which may conflict national constitutional rights and principles.[218] This can only be avoided by a certain level of harmonisation because even European fundamental rights do not necessarily cover all national constitutional rights. Originally, the *ordre public* is a reaction to differences between national legal systems and their application.[219] Consequently, the insufficient state of harmonisation within the EU still justifies a national *ordre public* concept as contained in Art. 34(1) Brussels I including the European *ordre public*.[220] This also seems to be the position of the European Parliament on the Proposal.[221] However, the objective should certainly

---

[214] Schlosser Report [1979] OJ C 59/71, p. 128.

[215] Magnus/Mankowski/*Franq*, Art. 34 para. 35.

[216] Cf. in detail *Basedow* in FS für Sonnenberger, p. 291; *Bach*, Grenzüberschreitende Vollstreckung, p. 109.

[217] *Leible*, ecolex 2011, p. 709; *Oberhammer*, IPRax 2010, p. 202 calls this "not quite European".

[218] *Garcia*, YPIL 2010, p. 371.

[219] *Martiny* in FS für Sonnenberger, p. 539.

[220] *Georganti*, Ordre public, p. 150; *Sujecki*, ZEuP 2008, p. 476; *Fabian*, Europäische Mahnverordnung, p. 316.

[221] European Parliament, Draft Report of 26 June 2011 (2010/0383(COD)), p. 28.

in the long run be a Europeanised standard – not confined to the right to a fair trial – entailing the benefit of a uniform interpretation by the ECJ.

f) Procedure in the Member State of enforcement

Art. 46 Proposal provides for a special remedy to a court of the enforcement Member State. Given the importance of ensuring compliance with Art. 47 of the Charter, the introduction of a special remedy must be endorsed. Relying solely on remedies available under the non-harmonised national enforcement laws would risk a lack of protection and entail significant uncertainty. However, one would have expected a remedy in the Member State of origin because the Commission continuously emphasised the objective to reduce intermediate measures and the principle of mutual recognition (Art. 67(4) TFEU).[222] Mutual recognition implies that it is not justified to impose controls in a Member State when they have already been carried out in another Member State.[223] It would therefore be incompatible to deny enforcement using the (national) *ordre public* if the reason for the breach is a rule that should have been applied in the Member State of origin.[224] This is the case with the European right to a fair trial. Moreover, with this rule being the same in all Member States, there is in theory no reason why the courts in the Member State of enforcement should be better placed to ensure its "correct" application.[225] However, mutual trust is still a postulate. In practice it seems unrealistic that a judgment would be reviewed equally critical in the Member State of origin.[226] In a case like *Krombach,* where the process complied with national law but violated Art. 6 ECHR, it seems much less likely that review by a court of the same State would bring about a different result, i.e. there is a likely structural bias in the Member State of origin. Furthermore, if the *ordre public* concept of Art. 34(1) Brussels I would be maintained – as ultimately argued above – a review in the Member State of origin would be impracticable. The court would have to assess every judgment against the diverging *ordre publics* of all other (potential enforcement) Member States and face expensive enquiries on their content. Since they are identified by the courts on a case-by-case basis accompanied by intense academic discussion, there is no ex-

---

[222] Recital 2 Proposal; Explanatory Memorandum, COM(2010) 748 final, paras. 1.2. and 3.1.1.
[223] *Garcia*, YPIL 2010, p. 363; *Cuniberti*, 14 Colum.J.Eur.L. 2007/08, p. 372; *Hess*, Europäisches Zivilprozessrecht, p. 95.
[224] *Garcia*, YPIL 2010, p. 370.
[225] *Oberhammer*, IPRax 2010, p. 202.
[226] *Cuniberti/Rueda*, RabelsZ 2011, p. 312; on the EEO *Dicey/Morris/Collins*, Conflict of Laws I, para. 14-233.

haustive set of rules which could be consulted. Hence, a review in the enforcement Member State is the only reasonable solution.

It is submitted the *ordre public* defence should only be available if the defendant has exhausted all means of redress in the Member State of origin. Whereas this is only commonly accepted for procedural fraud,[227] it is a general rule applied to Art. 34(1) Brussels I in Germany.[228] Art. 46 Proposal does not express this condition but it may be inferred from recital 24 Proposal characterising it as an 'extraordinary' remedy.[229] Nevertheless, an express rule should be adopted to enhance legal certainty.

g) Interim conclusion

For the fundamental rights reasons and the insufficient state of harmonisation it must be appreciated that the Commission did not continue its course of abolishing the *ordre public* defence. However, Art. 46(1) Proposal should be amended considerably. The protection of European fundamental rights should not be limited to the right to a fair trial. This is only one of several reasons to maintain the substantive *ordre public*. Moreover, the time does not seem ripe to rely solely on a European *ordre public*. In sum, the position of the European Parliament must be endorsed that the *ordre public* defence of Art. 34(1) Brussels I should be maintained.[230] A continuing restrictive interpretation in conjunction with the new procedural framework should suffice to enhance efficiency. If the defence is raised in a case of a breach of European fundamental rights the court in the enforcement state is obliged to refuse enforcement according to the submitted fundamental rights obligation.[231] This result can be based, either on an interpretation of "shall be refused" in Art. 46(5) Proposal as granting a discretion only in so far as the Member State's public interests or objective principles are concerned, or by accepting a general discretion, in the exercise of which the Member States are bound directly by European fundamental rights to refuse enforcement.[232]

---

[227] Cf. *Hess/Pfeiffer/Schlosser*, Heidelberg Report, paras. 481-490.

[228] BGH (German Federal Court of Justice) NJW 1990, 2201; *Kropholler/von Hein*, Art. 34 EuGVO para. 14.

[229] Suggested by *Hess*, IPRax 2011, p. 128.

[230] European Parliament, Draft Report of 26 June 2011 (2010/0383(COD)), p. 28.

[231] Like this *Basedow* in FS für Sonnenberger, p.316; *Becker*, Grundrechtsschutz, p. 132.

[232] *Fawcett* suggests a new two stage approach with a mandatory fundamental rights consideration at the first stage to achieve the same result with the *ordre public* defence at the second stage, ICLQ 2007, p. 43 et seq.

II. Natural Justice

1. Art. 34(2) Brussels I Regulation

According to Art. 34(2) Brussels I enforcement of a foreign default judgment shall be refused, if the defendant was not served with the documents which instituted the proceedings or with an equivalent document in sufficient time and in such a way as to arrange for his defence, unless he failed to challenge the judgment when it was possible for him to do so. Although, this is referred to as the 'natural justice defence' it must be distinguished from the Common Law conflict of laws defence.[233] Art. 34(2) Brussels I is a special *ordre public* defence protecting the defendant's right to be heard already during the commencement of proceedings. It is entirely dedicated to the circumstances enabling the defendant to organise for his defence before the court of origin and thus serves a complementary role to the protection already afforded by Art. 26 Brussels I at the jurisdiction stage. As opposed to its predecessor (Art. 27(2) Brussels Convention), it does not require the cumulation of service in sufficient time and in a sufficient way, resulting in increased protection. Moreover, formal regularity of service is not required as long as it *in fact* enables the defendant to arrange his defence.[234] However, the proviso of exhausted means of redress in the State of origin also restricted the scope of protection. Since, in practice, this is the most important defence[235] the ECJ has been concerned with its interpretation several times and the established case law solved most questions on its application.[236]

2. Art. 45 Proposal

Art. 45(1) Proposal provides a special remedy for a debtor of a default judgment in the Member State of *origin* when (a) the *same conditions* as under Art. 34(2) Brussels I are given, *or* (b) the defendant was prevented from contesting the claim by reason of *force majeure* or due to extraordinary circumstances without any fault on his part; the proviso of Art. 34(2) Brussels I applies to both scenar-

---

[233] cf. *Cheshire/North/Fawcett*, Private International Law, p. 563 et seqq. and 615 et seqq.

[234] Case C-283/05 ASML Netherlands BV v Semiconductor Industry Services GmbH (SEMIS) [2006] ECR I-12041, paras. 41-47; cf. *Cheshire/North/Fawcett*, Private International Law, p. 618.

[235] *Hess/Pfeiffer/Schlosser*, Heidelberg Report, para. 474.

[236] Cf. *inter alia* Case 166/80 *Klomps v Michel* [1981] ECR I-1593; Case C-172/91 *Volker Sonntag v Waidmann* [1993] ECR I-1963; Case C-78/95 *Hendrikman v Magenta Druck & Verlag GmbH* [1996] ECR I-4943.

ios. The defendant must apply to the competent court using the form set out in Annex II Proposal.

3. Discussion

In the light of the objective of free movement of judgements, it surprises that there is no discussion on the abolishment of the natural justice defence. *Krombach* clarified that there is a *lex specialis* relationship to the *ordre public* defence – which would equal apply to Art. 46 Proposal – as the latter includes the general right to a fair trial. Hence, it could be argued there is no need for this additional defence. Art. 34(2) Brussels I pointed out to the Member States the importance of this particular aspect of the defendant's right to be heard for decades which may suffice for a consideration under Art. 46 Proposal. If the recitals expressed this incorporation, the present case law could remain applicable. However, the European legislator obviously does not share this view.

Unlike for the *ordre public* defence, the Commission plans only a marginal substantive reform of the natural justice defence. The introduction of the additional reason of Art. 45(1)(b) Proposal further increases the protection of the defendant. The Proposal contains no explanation as to the precise meaning of the terms 'force majeure' and 'extraordinary circumstances'. They should be interpreted autonomously and in line with the corresponding provision in other regulations.[237] Cases of *force majeure* require an event entirely beyond the control of the defendant, for example, a natural disaster.[238] Art. 45(1)(b) Proposal enables the court to consider special circumstances which occurred after service took place. It seems reasonable to protect the defendant's right to be heard also in such cases since he is not least affected than in the situation of Art. 45(1)(a) Proposal. Given the narrow scope of this defence, the creditor's position is not significantly impaired. Thus it surprises that the European Parliament rejects its introduction.[239]

The most significant reform proposal is the shift of the review procedure to the Member State of origin.

---

[237] *Inter alia* Art. 19(1)(b) Regulation 4/2009; Art. 19(1)(b) Regulation 805/2004; Art. 18(1)(b) Regulation 861/2007.

[238] Cf. Rauscher/*Andrae/Schimrick*, Art. 19 EG-UntVO para. 19.

[239] Cf. European Parliament, Draft Report of 26 June 2011 (2010/0383(COD)), p. 28.

a) No minimum standard review approach

The wording of Art. 45(1) Proposal corresponds with Art. 19 Regulation 4/2009 relating to maintenance obligations. As mentioned earlier, some of the other regulations introduced minimum standards to ensure compliance with the specific aspect of the right to a fair trial covered by the natural justice defence.[240] These minimum standards served as a reasonable basis for mutual trust, justifying the shift of review of the European Enforcement Order or the particular certified judgment to the Member State of origin.[241] However, Regulation 4/2009 – now followed by Art. 45(1) Proposal – was the first regulation not to continue this approach. The separating of procedural minimum harmonisation and the shift of the review to the Member State of origin appears critical, as it eliminates the basis for mutual trust. It might be argued that such minimum standards exist in all national procedural laws as a consequence of the prior regulations. However, this is in fact not guaranteed because the adoption of their regime was not mandatory but optional. Only Member States which opted for providing some of their national titles with more freedom in the EU "had to pay the price of minimum harmonisation".[242] In order to create a uniform basis of mutual trust for this particular aspect of the defendant's right, the Proposal should adopt similar minimum standards of service.[243]

b) Procedure in the Member State of origin

The shift of the review procedure to the Member State of origin is a further step in the Commission's plan to reduce intermediate measures in the Member State of enforcement and to realise the principle of mutual recognition. The Member State of enforcement is prohibited from reviewing compliance of the judgment with natural justice, but rather must recognise the positive decision of the court in the Member State of origin. The introduction of this 'one-stop-shop' clearly benefits the defendant, because it eliminates the time consuming and costly multiple reviews in each enforcement state and the risk of diverging results.[244] The state of origin will often be the defendant's home state, i.e. proceedings will be less burdensome, because of the general jurisdiction rule of Art. 3 Proposal (Art.

---

[240] Cf. Chapter III Regulation 805/2004; Art. 13-15 Regulation 1896/2006; Art. 13 Regulation 861/2007.

[241] With respect to the EEO *Rechberger* in FS für Leipold, p. 305; *Fiorini*, ICLQ 2008, p. 451 et seq.

[242] *Leible*, ecolex 2011, p. 710.

[243] *Hess*, IPRax 2011, p. 99; *Leible*, ecolex 2011, p. 711; arguably also *Cheshire/North/ Fawcett*, Private International Law, p. 649.

[244] With respect to the EEO, cf. *Oberhammer*, JBl. 2006, p. 485.

2 Brussels I). Nevertheless, since neither the Commission nor the European Parliament[245] seem to be willing to introduce procedural minimum standards, this potentially beneficial shift lacks the necessary basis of mutual trust and again raises the concern of a likely structural bias in the Member State of origin. The European legislator should either introduce minimum standards or maintain the review in the Member State of enforcement; both approaches entail certain benefits. At any rate Art. 45 Proposal should be amended. The European Parliament argues for the second approach which allows a consolidated procedure for the different defences and thus also for a reduction of procedural costs compared to the current proposal.

III. Irreconcilable Judgments

1. Art. 34(3), (4) Brussels I Regulation and Art. 43 Proposal

Art. 34(3), (4) Brussels I provide that, under certain conditions, a judgment is not enforced if it is irreconcilable with a judgment given in the Member State of enforcement (3), or with an earlier judgment from another Member State or a third State (4). Whereas Art. 34(3) provides strict preference for judgments of the Member State of enforcement, Art. 34(4) contains a priority rule for conflicts with judgments of another origin. Judgments are irreconcilable when they entail consequences which are mutually exclusive.[246] These grounds of refusal are mandatory, i.e. the court has no discretion to assess the level of disturbance caused by the coexistence of the two judgments.[247] They are concerned with the rule of law in the addressed Member State and the smooth functioning of the European area of justice rather than the protection of individual parties.[248] Like Art. 34(2) Brussels I, they serve a complementary role, namely for the rules on *lis pendens* and related actions in Art. 27-3 0 Brussels I, which usually prevent the pursuit of proceedings before the court of two Member States when they are identical or related.[249]

---

[245] Cf. European Parliament, Draft Report of 26 June 2011 (2010/0383(COD)), p. 28.

[246] Case 145/86 *Hoffmann v Krieg* [1988] ECR I-645, para. 22.

[247] Case C-80/00 Italian Leather SpA v WECO Polstermöbel GmbH & Co. [2000] ECR I-4995, para. 52.

[248] Jenard Report [1979] OJ C 59/1, p. 45; *Kuipers*, CYELP 2010,p. 32; Magnus/Mankowski/*Franq*, Art.34 para. 60.

[249] Jenard Report [1979] OJ C 59/1, p. 45; cf. also *Cheshire/North/Fawcett*, Private International Law, p. 625.

Art. 43 Proposal provides for a special remedy to the competent *authority* in the enforcement Member State which, in substance, is *identical* to Art. 34(3), (4) Brussels I.

2. Discussion

Since the form of a special remedy is a mere consequence of the abolishment of the exequatur, the only real change envisaged by Art. 43 Proposal is the review by the enforcement authority rather than a court as in Art. 45 and 46 Proposal. Yet this shift and the lack of substantive reform raise concerns.

Before a discussion of these issues, it should be noted that, although these defences are not concerned with fundamental rights and thus there is no obligation to provide such a review, their necessity is undisputed. The Proposal's rules relating to *lis pendens* and related actions will again prevent most cases of irreconcilable judgments but in practice they will not always succeed.[250] Conflicting judgments from different Member States will still occur when the court is unaware of foreign proceedings because the parties do not raise the subject, i.e. especially in default proceedings.[251] Under the Brussels I, however, conflicts with judgments from third States – covered by Art. 34(4) – are even more likely since their proceedings are not considered in Art. 27-30. This is inconsistent with the objective of these rules to prevent irreconcilable judgments.[252] Since the court usually depends on objections by the parties, it should not actually be harder for the court to find out about proceedings in third States than in another Member State. Art. 34 Proposal now covers these proceedings. Therefore, it will make Art. 43(b) Proposal complementary in character and reduce the number of applications for this defence.

a) No general priority rule

Art. 43(a) Proposal adopts the approach of strict precedence of judgments from the Member State of origin. This has long been criticised by the *Heidelberg Report* and many commentators with respect to Brussels I, as it prefers a judgment given without respecting the *lis pendens* of the same lawsuit in another Member State. Such a rule is contrary to the general principle of equivalence of judgments in the European area of justice and thus an expression of obsolete nation-

---

[250] For an overview on the case law on Brussels I cf. Magnus/Mankowski/*Franq*, Art. 34 paras. 60 et seqq.

[251] Cf. Magnus/Mankowski/*Franq*, Art. 34 para. 61; *Kuipers*, CYELP 2010, p. 32.

[252] Cf. Case 144/86 *Gubisch Maschinenfabrik KG v Giulio Palumbo* [1987] ECR I-4861, para. 8.

alism.[253] It results in cases where effects of an earlier foreign judgment in the Member State of enforcement have to be annulled *ex nunc*.[254] This critique has been considered for the other regulations and resulted in the adoption of a general priority rule.[255] Art. 43 Proposal should be amended accordingly.[256] Furthermore, the *Heidelberg Report* argues for relying on the moment of pendency of the proceedings rather than the moment when the judgments are rendered.[257] This appears a better approach than the current Art. 43 Proposal because it would be consistent with Art. 29-34 Proposal. Moreover, an additional requirement that the pendency of the foreign proceedings or the irreconcilability could not have been sought in the original proceedings[258] would restrict the defence further and emphasise the general principle that protection must be sought primarily before the court of origin. Unfortunately, the adoption of any of these suggestions seems unlikely as the European Parliament also opts for keeping the defences as construed under Art. 34(3), (4) Brussels I.[259]

b) The competent authority in the Member State of enforcement

Art. 43 Proposal is the second remedy to be applied for in the Member State of enforcement. Given the current rule of Art. 43(a) Proposal, this is only reasonable. It would be impossible for a court in the Member State of origin to give preference to an enforcement State judgment when that State has not been identified yet. In case of several enforcement States, the remedy could be applied for more than once and the same court would have to give effect to different judgments. However, the other regulations suggest that even if a strict priority rule is adopted, it can be argued the Member State of enforcement is in the best position to assess whether another judgment would have to be recognised and might thus fulfil the requirements of the defence.[260]

The proposal provides no explanation for appointing the competent authority instead of a court to deal with the application. It has been pointed out above that

---

[253] *Oberhammer*, IPRax 2010, p. 202; *Hess*, Europäisches Zivilprozessrecht, p. 351; *Bach*, ZRP 2011, p. 99.

[254] *Kropholler*, Art. 34 EuGVO para. 54; *Leible/Freitag*, EU Forderungsbeitreibung, p. 153.

[255] Cf. Art. 21 Regulation 805/2004, Art. 22 Regulation 1896/2006, Art. 22 Regulation 861/2007.

[256] Like this *inter alia Hess*, IPRax 2011, p. 128; *Oberhammer*, IPRax 2010, p. 202.

[257] *Hess/Pfeiffer/Schlosser*, Heidelberg Report, para. 496.

[258] Ibid.

[259] Cf. European Parliament, Draft Report of 26 June 2011 (2010/0383(COD)), p. 28.

[260] *Oberhammer*, JBl. 2006, p. 496.

the national enforcement authority may not be a court. An example is the bailiff in Germany. The authority may lack a sufficient legal education. The case law and the academic discussion on Art. 34(3), (4) Brussels I are evidence for the difficulty of their application.[261] Therefore, Art. 43 Proposal must be amended. Shifting the competence to a court would also allow for a concentration of the defences in a uniform remedy to the same court,[262] which could establish specialist chambers. That would reduce procedural costs and increase the effectiveness of the debtor's defence considerably.

IV. Breach of certain rules on jurisdiction

1. Art. 35 Brussels I - abolished under the Proposal

Finally, Art. 35(1) Brussels I provides a defence when the court of origin assumed jurisdiction contrary to the rules of Brussels I for insurance or consumer contracts, heads of exclusive jurisdiction, or in a case provided for in Art. 72 (special international agreement prior to the Brussels I). It is an exception to the general principle in Art. 35(3) Brussels I that the jurisdiction of the court of origin may not be reviewed. According to the ECJ, a court of one Member State is generally not in a better position to determine whether the court of another Member State has jurisdiction.[263] In any case, the reviewing court is bound by the finding of facts on which the original court based its jurisdiction, Art. 35(2) Brussels I.

The Proposal entirely abolishes this defence.

2. Discussion

The Proposal follows the recommendation of the *Heidelberg Report,* according to which such a defence is not in line with the principle of mutual trust.[264] The latter is justified by the harmonised jurisdiction regime. The review concerns rules which already have to be applied by the court of origin, i.e. it also contra-

---

[261] Cf. Cheshire/North/Fawcett, Private International Law, p. 622 et seqq.; Magnus/Mankowski/*Franq*, Art. 34 paras. 60 et seqq.

[262] European Parliament, Draft Report of 26 June 2011 (2010/0383(COD)), p. 28; *Leible*, ecolex 2011, p. 709.

[263] Last in Case C-185/07 *Allianz SpA and Others v West Tankers Inc.* [2009] ECR I-663, para. 29.

[264] *Hess/Pfeiffer/Schlosser*, Heidelberg Report, para. 496.

dicts the principle of mutual recognition.[265] Nevertheless, some argue that insurance policy holders and consumers deserve special protection justifying a jurisdiction defence.[266] This policy statement adds little to the above criticism. When the *Heidelberg Report* argues Art. 35(1) Brussels I is inconsistent because it misses jurisdiction rules on employment contracts, it disregards that, unlike the included grounds, their consideration would not protect the usually weaker party. However, this argument does not explain the review of exclusive grounds of jurisdiction. At any rate, there is no apparent reason why the European Parliament suggests a defence only for the jurisdiction rules on consumer contracts.[267] It demonstrates that such a jurisdiction defence would be based on policy rather than legal principles. Unlike in Regulation 805/2005 and Regulation 1896/2006,[268] precisely this part of the defence on consumers was excluded from the subsequent Regulation 861/2007, i.e. special protection of consumers was regarded unnecessary. Ultimately, the harmonised rules on jurisdiction allow for the reliance on mutual trust so that mutual recognition should be demanded and the Proposal's abolishment of this defence must be endorsed.[269]

Art. 83 Proposal which is identical to Art. 72 Brussels I arguably suffices to prevent the enforcement of judgments contrary to respective international agreements because it provides that the latter prevails. An express defence should not be necessary.

[265] *Garcia*, YPIL 2011, p. 364 et seqq.

[266] *Schlosser*, IPRax 2010, p. 103; detailed with respect to consumers *Kieninger*, VuR 2011, p. 249.

[267] Cf. European Parliament, Draft Report of 26 June 2011 (2010/0383(COD)), p. 28.

[268] Cf. Art. 6(1)(d) Regulation 805/2004 and Art. 6(2) Regulation 1896/2006.

[269] Like this arguably also *Kropholler*, Art. 35 EuGVO para. 7; Rauscher/*Leible*, Art. 35 Brussels I para. 6.

E. Final Conclusion

It has been demonstrated that the reforms envisaged by the Proposal enhance the free movement of judgments and the realisation of the principle of mutual recognition. The fundamental change of the enforcement system by the general abolishment of the exequatur must be endorsed. Although, mutual trust is still a postulate requiring a 'leap in the dark', the economic benefits are convincing. The supplementing reforms, especially the extended standard form certificate, ensure that the import function of the exequatur will be compensated. The defences provided in the form of special remedies, however, should be amended. It is submitted that European fundamental rights require a fundamental rights review of the foreign judgment beyond the fair trial defence of Art. 46 Proposal. Moreover, the current state of harmonisation still necessitates the substantive *ordre public* and maintaining a national *ordre public* concept, even though, in the long run a European standard may be more appropriate. Art. 45 Proposal should be accompanied by the introduction of minimum standards for service. The adoption of a uniform priority rule in Art. 43 Proposal would eliminate existing inconsistency. The remedies in the Member State of enforcement should be centralised with specialised courts. Many of these amendments are supported by the European Parliament. They would increase the protection to the necessary level, and facilitate the efficiency of the defence regime. Finally, it can be concluded that the Proposal points in the right direction, but is nevertheless still improvable. It remains to be seen whether, in the further legislative process, providing the necessary protection can take preference over the aim of maximum efficiency, i.e. to what extent the Commission is ready to adopt the suggested amendments.

References

Articles

***Bach**, Ivo*

Drei Entwicklungsschritte im europäischen Zivilprozessrecht, Zeitschrift für Rechtspolitik 2011, p. 97 et seqq. (cit.: *Bach*, ZRP 2011, p...)

***Beaumont**, Paul/ **Johnston**, Emma*

Can *Exequatur* be abolished in Brussels I whilst retaining a public policy defence?, Journal of Private International Law 2010, p. 249 et seqq. (cit.: *Beaumont/Johnston*, J.Priv.Int.L. 2010, p...)

***Blobel**, Felix/ **Späth**, Patrick*

The tale of multilateral trust and the European law of civil procedure, European Law Review 2005, p. 528 et seqq. (cit.: *Blobel/Späth*, ELRev 2005, p...)

***Briggs**, Adrian*

Decisions of British Courts during 2004 – Private International Law, The British Year Book of International Law 2004, p.537 et seqq. (cit.: *Briggs*, BYBIL 2004, p...)

***Carruthers**, Janeen Margaret*

The Brussels I Regulation Recast, Scots Law Times 2011, p. 31 et seqq. (cit.: *Carruthers*, SLT 2011, p...)

***Correa Delcasso**, Juan Pablo*

Civil Enforcement in Spain, European Business Law Review 2006, p. 697 et seqq. (cit.: *Correa Delcasso*, EBLR 2006, p...)

***Crifo**, Carla*

First steps towards the harmonisation of civil procedure: the regulation creating a European enforcement order for uncontested claims, Civil Justice Quarterly 2005, p. 200 et seqq. (cit.: *Crifo*, CJQ 2005, p...)

***Cuniberti**, Gilles*

Debarment from Defending, Default Judgments and Public Policy, Praxis des Internationalen Privat- und Verfahrensrechts 2010, p. 148 et seqq. (cit.: *Cuniberti*, IPRax 2010, p...)

***Cuniberti**, Gilles*

The first stage of the abolition of the exequatur in the European Union, Columbia Journal of European Law 14 (2007/2008), p. 371 et seqq. (cit.: *Cuniberti*, 14 Colum.J.Eur.L. 2007/08, p...)

Cuniberti, Gilles

The recognition of foreign judgments lacking reason in Europe: Access to justice, foreign court avoidance, and efficiency, International and Comparative Law Quarterly 2008, p. 25 et seqq. (cit.: *Cuniberti*, ICLQ 2008, p...)

***Cuniberti**, Gilles/ **Rueda**, Isabella*

Abolition of Exequatur – Addressing the Commission's Concerns, Rabels Zeitschrift für ausländisches und internationals Privatrecht 2011, p.286 et seqq. (cit.: *Cuniberti/Rueda*, RabelsZ 2011, p...)

***Fawcett**, James J.*

The Impact of Art.6(1) of the ECHR on Private International Law, International and Comparative Law Quarterly 2007, p. 1 et seqq. (cit.: *Fawcett*, ICLQ 2007, p...)

***Fiorini**, Aude*

Facilitating cross-border debt recovery: the European payment order and small claims regulations, International & Comparative Law Quarterly 2008, p. 449 et seqq. (cit.: *Fiorini*, ICLQ 2008, p...)

***Garcia**, Rafael Arenas*

Abolition of exequatur: problems and solutions – mutual recognition, mutual trust and recognition of foreign judgments: too many words in the sea, Yearbook of Private International Law 2010, p. 351 et seqq. (cit.: *Garcia*, YPIL 2010, p...)

***Hess**, Burkhard*

Die Reform der EuGVVO und die Zukunft des Europäischen Zivilprozessrechts, Praxis des Internationalen Privat- und Verfahrensrechts 2011, p. 125 et seqq. (cit.: *Hess*, IPRax 2011, p...)

***Hess**, Burkhard/ **Bittmann**, David*

Die Effektuierung des Exequaturverfahrens nach der Europäischen Gerichtsstands- und Vollstreckungsverordnung, Praxis des Internationalen Privat- und Verfahrensrechts 2007, p. 277 et seqq. (cit.: *Hess/Bittmann*, IPRax 2007, p...)

***Hess**, Burkhard/ **Mack**, Marcus*

Civil Enforcement in Germany, European Business Law Review 2006, p. 655 et seqq. (cit.: *Hess/Mack*, EBLR 2006, p...)

***Kieninger**, Eva-Maria*

Die Abschaffung des Vollstreckbarerklärungs-verfahrens der EuGVVO und die Zukunft des Verbraucherschutzes, Verbraucher und Recht 2011, p. 243 et seqq. (cit.: *Kieninger*, VuR 2011, p...)

***Kinsch**, Patrick*

The Impact of Human Rights on the Application of Foreign Law and on the Recognition of Foreign Judgments – A Survey of the Cases Decided by the European Human Rights Institutions, in: Einhorn, Talia/ Siehr, Kurt (ed.), Intercontinental Cooperation Trough Private International Law – Essays in Memory of Peter E. Nygh (2004), T.M.C. Asser Press, The Hague (cit.: *Kinsch* in Einhorn/Siehr, Essays in Memory of Nygh, p...)

***Kohler**, Christian*

Von der EuGVVO zum Europäischen Vollstreckungstitel – Entwicklungen und Tendenzen im Recht der Anerkennung und Vollstreckung ausländischer Entscheidungen, in: Reichelt, Gerte/ Rechberger, Walter H. (ed.), Europäisches Kollisionsrecht (2004), Manzsche Verlags- und Universitätsbuchhandlung, Wien (cit.: *Kohler* in Reichelt/Rechberger (ed.), Europäisches Kollisionsrecht, p...)

***Kuipers**, Jan-Jaap*

The right to a fair trial and the free movement of civil judgments, Croatian Yearbook of European Law and Policy 2010, p. 23 et seqq. (cit.: *Kuipers*, CYELP 2010, p...)

***Leible**, Stefan*

Wegfall des Exequaturs und Änderung der Anerkennungsversagungsgründe im Vorschlag für eine Neufassung der Brüssel I-VO, Ecolex 2011, forthcoming (cit.: *Leible*, ecolex 2011, p...)

***Lock**, Tobias*

Beyond Bosphorus: the European Court of Human Rights' case law on the responsibility of member states of international organisations under the European Convention on Human Rights, Human Rights Law Review 2010, p. 529 et seqq. (cit.: *Lock*, HRLRev 2010, p...)

***Magnus**, Ulrich/ **Mankowski**, Peter*

Brussels I on the Verge of Reform – A Response to the Green Paper on the Review of the Brussels I Regulation, Zeitschrift für Vergleichende Rechtswissenschaft 2010, p. 1 et seqq. (cit.: *Magnus/Mankowski*, ZVglRWiss 109 (2010), p.)

***Matscher**, Franz*

Die indirekte Wirkung des Art. 6 EMRK bei der Anerkennung und Vollstreckung ausländischer Entscheidungen, in: Bork, Reinhard/ Hoeren, Thomas/ Pohlmann, Petra (ed.), Recht und Risiko – Festschrift für Helmut Kollhosser zum 70. Geburtstag (2004) Verlag Versicherungswirtschaft, Karlsruhe (cit.: *Matscher* in FS für Kollhosser II, p...)

***Meidanis**, Haris P.*

Public policy and *ordre public* in the private international law of the EC/EU: Traditional positions of the Member States and modern trends, European Law Review 2005, p. 95 et seqq. (cit.: *Meidanis*, ELRev 2005, p...)

***Oberhammer**, Paul*

Civil Enforcement in Austria, European Business Law Review 2006, p. 595 et seqq. (cit.: *Oberhammer*, EBLR 2006, p...)

***Oberhammer**, Paul*

Der Europäische Vollstreckungstitel: Rechtspolitische Ziele und Methoden, Juristische Blätter 2006, p. 477 et seqq. (cit.: *Oberhammer*, JBl. 2006, p...)

***Oberhammer**, Paul*

The Abolition of Exequatur, Praxis des Internationalen Privat- und Verfahrensrechts 2010, p. 197 et seqq. (cit.: *Oberhammer*, IPRax 2010, p...)

***Rechberger**, Walter H.*

Die neue Generation – Bemerkungen zu den Verordnungen Nr. 805/2004, Nr. 1896/2006 und Nr. 861/2007 des Europäischen Parlaments und des Rates, In: Festschrift für Dieter Leipold zum 70. Geburtstag, 2009, p. 301 et seqq., Mohr Siebeck, Tübingen (cit.: *Rechberger* in FS für Leipold, p...)

***Schack**, Heimo*

The Misguided Abolition of Exequatur Proceedings in the European Union, in: Festschrift für Tadeusz Erecinski 2011, forthcoming (cit.: *Schack* in FS für Erecinski, forthcoming)

***Schilling**, Theodor*

Das Exequatur und die EMRK, Praxis des Internationalen Privat- und Verfahrensrechts 2011, p. 31 et seqq. (cit.: *Schilling*, IPRax 2011, p...)

***Stein**, Andreas*

Der Europäische Vollstreckungstitel für unbestrittene Forderungen tritt in Kraft – Aufruf zu einer nüchternen Betrachtung, Praxis des Internationalen Privat- und Verfahrensrechts 2004, p. 181 et seqq. (cit.: *Stein*, IPRax 2004, p...)

***Sujecki**, Bartosz*

Die Möglichkeiten und Grenzen der Abschaffung des ordre public-Vorbehalts im Europäischen Zivilprozessrecht, Zeitschrift für Europäisches Privatrecht 2008, p.458 et seqq.(cit.: *Sujecki*, ZEuP 2008, p...)

Wagner, Rolf/ **Beckmann**, Martina
Beibehaltung oder Abschaffung des Vollstreckbarerklärungsverfahrens in der EuGVVO?, Recht der Internationalen Wirtschaft 2011, p. 44 et seqq. (cit.: *Wagner/Beckmann*, RIW 2011, p...)

Reports

***Jenard**, Paul*
Report on the Convention on jurisdiction and the enforcement of judgments in civil and commercial matters [1979] OJ C 59/1 (cit.: Jenard Report [1979] OJ C 59/1, p...)

***Schlosser**, Peter*
Report on the Convention on the Association of the Kingdom of Denmark, Ireland and the United Kingdom of Great Britain and Northern Ireland to the Convention on jurisdiction and the enforcement of judgments in civil and commercial matters and to the Protocol on its interpretation by the Court of Justice [1979] OJ C 59/71 (cit.: Schlosser Report [1979] OJ C 59/71, p...)

Books

***Bach**, Ivo*
Grenzüberschreitende Vollstreckung in Europa, 1st edition, 2008, Mohr Siebeck, Tübingen (cit.: *Bach*, Grenzüberschreitende Vollstreckung, p...)

***Becker**, Ulrich*
Grundrechtsschutz bei der Anerkennung und Vollstreckbarerklärung im europäischen Zivilverfahrensrecht, 1st edition, 2004, Peter Lang, Frankfurt (cit.: *Becker*, Grundrechtsschutz, p...)

***Briggs**, Adrian/ **Rees**, Peter*
Civil Jurisdiction and Judgments, 5th edition, 2009, Informa Law, Zug (Switzerland),(cit.: *Briggs/Rees*, Civil Jurisdiction and Judgments, p...)

***Castel**, Jean-Gabriel/ **Walker**, Janet*
Canadian Conflict of Laws, 6th edition, 2005, LexisNexis Butterworths, Markham (cit.: *Castel/Walker*, Canadian Conflict of Laws, para.)

***Chalmers**, Damian/ **Davies**, Gareth/ **Monti**, Georgio*
European Union Law, 2nd edition, 2010, Cambridge University Press, Cambridge (cit.: *Chalmers/Davies/Monti*, EU Law, p...)

***Dicey**, Albert Venn/ **Morris**, John Humphrey Carlile/ **Collins**, Lawrence Antony*
The Conflict of Laws – Volume 1, 14th edition, 2006, Sweet & Maxwell, London (cit.: *Dicey/Morris/Collins*, Conflict of Laws I, para...)

***Fabian**, Anna-Katharina*
Die Europäische Mahnverfahrensverordnung im Kontext der Europäisierung des Prozessrechts, 1st edition, 2009, Jenaer Wissenschaftliche Verlagsgesellschaft, Jena (cit.: *Fabian*, Europäische Mahnverordnung, p...)

***Fawcett**, James J./ **Carruthers**, Janeen M.*
Cheshire, North & Fawcett – Private, International Law, 14th edition, 2008, Oxford University Press, Oxford (cit.: *Cheshire/North/Fawcett*, Private International Law, p...)

***Frowein**, Jochen/ **Peukert**, Wolfgang*
Europäische Menschenrechtskonvention, 3rd edition, 2009, N.P. Engel Verlag, Kehl (cit.: Frowein/Peukert/*Commentator*, Art... EMRK, para...)

***Georganti**, Philia*
Die Zukunft des ordre public-Vorbehalts im Europäischen Zivilprozessrecht, 1st edition, 2006, Herbert Utz Verlag, Munich (cit.: *Georganti*, Ordre public, p...)

***Harris**, David/ **O'Boyle**, Michael/ **Warbrick**, Colin*
Law of the European Convention on Human Rights, 2nd edition, 2009, Oxford University Press, Oxford (cit.: *Harris/O'Boyle/Warbrick*, ECHR, p...)

***Heringer**, Anja*
Der europäische Vollstreckungstitel für unbestrittene Forderungen, 1st edition, 2007, Nomos Verlagsgesellschaft, Baden-Baden (cit.: *Heringer*, Europäischer Vollstreckungstitel, p...)

Hess, Burkhard
Europäisches Zivilprozessrecht, 1st edition, 2010, C.F. Müller, Heidelberg (cit.: *Hess*, Europäisches Zivilprozessrecht, p...)

Hess, Burkhard/ **Pfeiffer**, Thomas/ **Schlosser**, Peter
The Brussels I-Regulation (EC) No 44/2001, The Heidelberg Report on the Application of Regulation Brussels I in 25 Member States (Study JLS/C4/2005/03), 2008
C.H. Beck, Munich (cit.: *Hess/Pfeiffer/Schlosser*, Heidelberg Report, para...)

***Kropholler**, Jan/ **von Hein**, Jan*
Europäisches Zivilprozessrecht – Kommentar zu EuGVO, Lugano-Übereinkommen 2007, EuVTVO, EuMVVO und EuGFVO, 9th edition, 2011, Verlag Recht und Wirtschaft, Frankfurt am Main (cit.: *Kropholler/von Hein*, Art... *Statute* para...)

***Layton**, Alexander/ **Mercer**, Hugh*
European Civil Practice – Volume I, 2nd edition, 2004, Sweet & Maxwell, London (cit.: *Layton/Mercer*, EU Civil Practice I, para...)

***Leible**, Stefan/ **Freitag**, Robert*
Forderungsbeitreibung in der EU, 1st edition, 2008, C.H. Beck, Munich (cit.: *Leible/Freitag*, EU Forderungsbeitreibung, p...)

***Magnus**, Ulrich/ **Mankowski**, Peter*
Brussels I Regulation, 1st edition, 2007, Sellier – European Law Publishers, Munich (cit.: Magnus/Mankowski/*Commentator*, Art... para...)

***Rauscher**, Thomas*
Der Europäische Vollstreckungstitel für unbestrittene Forderungen, 1st edition, 2004, Sellier – European Law Publishers, Munich (cit.: *Rauscher*, Europäischer Vollstreckungstitel, p...)

***Rauscher**, Thomas*
Europäisches Zivilprozess- und Kollisionsrecht (EuZPR/ EuIPR) – Brüssel I-VO, LugÜbk 2007, 1st edition, 2011, Sellier – European Law Publishers, Munich (cit.: Rauscher/*Commentator*, Art... Brussels I para...)

***Rauscher**, Thomas*
Europäisches Zivilprozess- und Kollisionsrecht (EuZPR/ EuIPR) – Brüssel IIa-VO, EG-UnthVO, EG-ErbVO-E, HUntStProt 2007, 1st edition, 2010, Sellier – European Law Publishers, Munich (cit.: Rauscher/*Commentator*, Art... *Statute* para...)

***Rauscher**, Thomas*
Europäisches Zivilprozess- und Kollisionsrecht (EuZPR/ EuIPR) – EG-VollstrTitelVO, EG-MahnVO, EG-BagatellVO, EG-ZustVO 2007, EG-BewVO, EG-InsVO, 1st edition, 2010, Sellier – European Law Publishers, Munich (cit.: Rauscher/*Commentator*, Art... *Statute* para...)

***Rauscher**, Thomas*
Internationales Privatrecht, 3rd edition, 2009, C.F. Müller, Heidelberg, Munich (cit.: *Rauscher*, Internationales Privatrecht, p...)

***Seidl**, Sandra*
Ausländische Vollstreckungstitel und inländischer Bestimmtheitsgrundsatz, 1st edition, 2010, Jenaer Wissenschaftliche Verlagsgesellschaft, Jena (cit.: *Seidl*, Vollstreckung und Bestimmtheitsgrundsatz., p...)

***Thoma**, Ionna*
Die Europäisierung und die Vergemeinschaftung des nationalen ordre public, 1st edition, 2007, Mohr Siebeck, Tübingen (cit.: *Thoma*, Europäisierung des ordre public, p...)

Cases

European Union

Case C-185/07 *Allianz SpA and Others v West Tankers Inc.* [2009] ECR I-663

Case C-283/05 ASML Netherlands BV v Semiconductor Industry Services GmbH (SEMIS) [2006] ECR I-12041

Case 125/79 *Denilauler v SNC Couchet Frèreres* [1980] ECR I-1553

Case 148/84 *Deutsche Genossenschaftsbank v Brasserie du pêcheur SA* [1985] ECR I-1981

Case C-128/97 *Eco Swiss China Time v Benetton International* [1999] ECR-3055

Case C-116/02 *Erich Gasser GmbH v Misat Srl.* [2004] ECR I-14693

Case C-394/07 *Gambazzi v DaimlerCrysler Canada Inc. and CIBC Mellon Trust Company* [2009] ECR I-2569

Case 144/86 *Gubisch Maschinenfabrik KG v Giulio Palumbo* [1987] ECR I-4861

Case C-524/06 *Heinz Huber v Germany* [2008] ECR I-9705, paras.74 et seq.

Case C-78/95 *Hendrikman v Magenta Druck & Verlag GmbH* [1996] ECR I-4943

Case 145/86 *Hoffmann v Krieg* [1988] ECR I-645

Case 12/76 *Industrie Tessili Italiana Como v Dunlop AG* [1976] ECR I-1473

Case C-80/00 *Italian Leather SpA v WECO Polstermöbel GmbH & Co.* [2000] ECR I-4995

Case C-491/10 *Joseba Andoni Aguirre Zarraga v Simone Pelz* (yet unreported in the ECR)

Case 166/80 *Klomps v Michel* [1981] ECR I-1593

Case C-7/98 *Krombach v Bamberski* [2000] ECR I-1935

Case 29/76 *Lufttransportunternehmen GmbH & Co. KG v Eurocontrol* [1976] ECR I-1541

Case 814/79 *Netherlands State v Rüffer* [1980] ECR I-3807

Case 4/73 *Nold v Commission* [1974] ECR I-491

Case C-305/05 *Ordre des barreaux francophones et germanophone v Conseil des ministres* [2007] ECR I-5305

Case 120/78 *Rewe-Zentral AG v Bundesmonopolverwaltung für Branntwein (Cassis de Dijon)* [1979] ECR I-649

Case C-159/02 *Turner v Grovit* [2005] ECR I-3565

Case C-172/91 *Volker Sonntag v Waidmann* [1993] ECR I-1963

Case 5/88 *Wachauf v Germany* [1989] ECR 2609

European Court of Human Rights

Bosphorus Hava Yollari Turizm ve Ticaret Anonim Sirketi v Ireland, No. 45036/98 (2005) 42 EHRR 1

Delcourt v Belgium, No. 2689/65 (1970) 1 EHRR 255

Drozd and Janousek v France and Spain, No. 12747/87 (1992) 14 EHRR 745

Golder v United Kingdom, No. 4451/70 (1975) 1 EHRR 524

Krombach v France, No. 29731/96 (2001) 12 HR Case Digest 76

Pauger v Austria, No. 16717/90 (1997) 25 EHRR 105

Pellegrini v Italy, No. 30882/96 (2001) 35 EHRR 44

Soering v United Kingdom, No. 14038/88 (1992) 14 EHRR 745

France

Court de cassation, Civ. 1ére, 30 juin 2004, *Stolzenberg c. CIBC Mellon Trust*, IPRax 2006, p.300

Germany

BGH (German Federal Court of Justice) EuZW 2007, 187

BGH (German Federal Court of Justice) IPRax 1994, 118 – *Volker Sonntag*

BGH (German Federal Court of Justice) NJW 1990, 2201

BGH (German Federal Court of Justice) NJW 1991, 1410

BGH (German Federal Court of Justice) NJW 2000, 3289

BGH (German Federal Court of Justice) NJW 2004, 2388

BGH (German Federal Court of Justice) NJW 2009, 3306

BVerfG (German Constitutional Court), BVerfGE 73, 339, *Re the application of Wünsche Handelsgesellschaft (Solange II)* [1987] 3 C.M.L.R. 225

United Kingdom

Government of the United States of America v Montgomery (No 2) [2004] 1 WLR 2241

Maronier v Lamer [2003] QB 620

United States of America

Lee v Winston, 1983, 717 F.2d 888 (Va.)

Fraguela v Fraguela, 1991, 576 N.Y.S.2d 669